Helen Gries

THE ISHTAR GATE OF BABYLON

From Fragment to Monument

Vorderasiatisches Museum
Staatliche Museen zu Berlin

SCHNELL + STEINER

CONTENTS

INTRODUCTION

The Ishtar Gate is a masterpiece of Babylonian architecture and the highlight of any visit to the *Vorderasiatisches Museum* (Museum of the Ancient Near East) on Museum Island in Berlin. Above all, it carries great symbolic significance for contemporary Iraq. Yet the gate may be interpreted quite differently, depending on the individual observer's perspective and background. This publication seeks to illuminate these different perspectives and focuses on the historical context of the discovery and reconstruction of the gate itself, as well as the respective actors and various motivations involved.

The Ishtar Gate brings multiple narratives together in a single monument. The first narrative is that of its creation in the 6th century BCE, under the Babylonian king Nebuchadnezzar II (604–562 BCE). In the heyday of the Babylonian Empire, Nebuchadnezzar II carried out enormous building projects in Babylon – including the Ishtar Gate, its adjoining Processional Way (Fig. 1), and the so-called Throne Room Façade in the royal palace. The gate's brightly coloured glazed bricks are masterpieces of craftsmanship and art. During the annual New Year celebrations – the most important religious festival in Babylonia – the processions of the gods entered the city centre through the Ishtar Gate.

The second narrative is that of the archaeological rediscovery of Babylon resulting from the excavation undertaken by the *Deutsche Orient-Gesellschaft* (German Oriental Society) from 1899 to 1917, under Robert Koldewey's direction. At that time, Babylon lay in the Ottoman Empire‹s territory. No part of the iteration of the Ishtar Gate that has been reconstructed in Berlin was still standing at that time. Only the earliest construction phase – a gate made of unglazed relief bricks – had been preserved and was still standing. Visitors can still see this phase in Babylon today. In addition, the archaeologists found thousands of small glazed-brick fragments in the rubble. These had once been part of another gate structure, which was decorated with colourful reliefs depicting animals. The team excavating the site systematically collected these fragments and later obtained permission to bring them to Germany.

The third narrative is that of the gate's reconstruction in Berlin in the 1920s. Before the painstaking assembly of the brick fragments could begin, the pieces required elaborate preparation. Since the original brick fragments were insufficient to reconstruct the entire Ishtar Gate, the then-director of the *Vorderasiatische Abteilung* (Department of the Ancient Near East), Walter Andrae, decided to fill in the gaps with new bricks made especially for this purpose. To this end, he commissioned three well-known ceramic manufacturers from the area around Berlin to produce suitable glazed bricks.

Ever since the Pergamon Museum opened its doors in 1930, the Ishtar Gate has fascinated visitors with its vivid colours; it has become a symbol of ancient Near Eastern architecture and art. In 1999, UNESCO designated Museum

Fig. 1: One of the lions along the Processional Way.

Island and its five museums as a World Heritage Site. Almost 20 years later, the same body also added the ancient city of Babylon to its list of World Heritage Sites, thus recognising Babylon's global importance. Since then, UNESCO has been committed to preserving both the remains of the Ishtar Gate that still stand in Babylon and the reconstruction of the gate in Berlin.

The Ishtar Gate is more than simply a historical monument to a bygone culture. Since its excavation and reconstruction, it has become an identity marker for the modern Iraqi state, which was founded in 1921. In this way, it is also part of our current societal discourse on how to address both Germany's and Europe's colonial past. Thus its story is not yet complete.

THE CITY OF BABYLON

A BRIEF HISTORY OF BABYLON

The city of Babylon is situated 85 kilometres south of Baghdad in present-day Iraq, in a landscape shaped by the Euphrates River. The alluvial plain around Babylon is very fertile, but its irrigation depends solely on rivers and canals. A branch of the Euphrates flowed through the midst of the ancient metropolis, dividing it into two urban areas.

Compared to other cities in southern Mesopotamia – such as Uruk, a settlement that dates back to the 5th millennium BCE – Babylon is a relatively young city. A small number of pottery sherds are all that attest to the site's settlement as early as the middle of the 3rd millennium BCE. We know little about the city's beginnings, however, since the groundwater level – which had risen sharply due to dam construction – prevented the exploration of the oldest archaeological layers in Babylon as early as the end of the 19th century. The city played neither a political nor a cultural role in the 3rd and early 2nd millennia BCE. Moreover, early written sources hardly mention Babylon.

This changed in the 18th century BCE, when King Hammurabi (ca. 1792–1750 BCE) expanded his territory considerably and Babylon consequently rose from a rather insignificant city-state to become the capital of a great kingdom. Over the course of his more than 40-year reign, the area under Hammurabi's control grew until it extended from the Persian Gulf all the way to Syria, thus establishing Babylon's supremacy in the ancient Near East. Under Hammurabi, the city developed into a centre for Mesopotamian scholarship, poetry, and art, and it remained so for almost 2,000 years. However, political dominance receded soon after Hammurabi's death. The great kingdom began to disintegrate under the rule of his son Samsuiluna (ca. 1750–1712 BCE), but it was the Hittite king Mursili I (ca. 1620–1590 BCE) who finally ended the Hammurabi dynasty's rule. He led his army from Anatolia to Babylon, conquering and then sacking the city. In terms of archaeology, we know very little about Babylon's first heyday under Hammurabi, as the archaeological layers corresponding to this era are submerged under the groundwater.

We also have little information about the 100 years or so after the Hittite raid. In the 15th century BCE, the Kassite dynasty advanced into the power vacuum created by the fall of the Old Babylonian kingdom. At first their sphere of influence was limited to Babylon, but over the course of the 14th century BCE, the Kassites gradually brought all of southern Mesopotamia and even Dilmun – what is today Bahrain in the Persian Gulf – under their control. Archaeologists have uncovered several private dwellings and numerous tombs from the Kassite era in settlement layers in the area of Babylon's central district.

In 1158 BCE, the Elamite king Shutruk-Nahhunte (ca. 1185–1155 BCE) brought more than

400 years of Kassite rule to an end when he led a military campaign into southern Mesopotamia and conquered the city of Babylon, among others. Elamite troops plundered the Babylonian temples. They carried off important works of art, including the Code of Hammurabi (Fig. 2), and brought them to their capital, Susa – what is today Shush in south-western Iran. Over the following decades, the Elamite army repeatedly moved into Babylonia, but Elam did not succeed in gaining permanent control over the region. The Elamite spoils of war included the ritual image of Marduk, Babylon's city god. This loss was particularly devastating for the population, as the statue of the god was considered the personification of the god, and thus the city was left without divine protection.

In these troubled times, a new dynasty was gaining strength in the city of Isin and increasingly came to dominate Babylonia. These kings moved their official residence from Isin to Babylon, linking their dynasty to the long reign of the Babylonian kings. King Nebuchadnezzar I (ca. 1125–1104 BCE) succeeded in conquering Susa and bringing the ritual statue of the god Marduk back to Babylon. The kings of Isin subsequently expanded their kingdom until it encompassed all of southern Mesopotamia, but their reign only lasted about 100 years. At the turn from the 2nd to the 1st millennium BCE, the Kingdom of Babylon once again disintegrated.

While the Kassites ruled in southern Mesopotamia from the 14th century BCE, the Assyrians were growing strong in northern Mesopotamia. From the 1st millennium BCE, Assyria dominated the region from the Persian Gulf to the Mediterranean. From then on, a tense, complicated relationship existed between Babylonia and Assyria, characterised by Assyria's military superiority and Babylon's traditional position as a centre of religion, culture, and scholarship. Some of the Assyrian kings even held the prestigious title "king of Babylon". Babylonian–Assyrian relations reached a blood-soaked low point under Sennacherib (704–681 BCE). When he ascended to the throne after his father Sargon II (721–705 BCE), the Babylonians did not accept him. In order to secure his rule over Babylon despite this resistance, he installed his son as regent in Babylon, but after a few years his son was expelled to Elam and was probably killed there. Most likely as revenge for his son's murder, over the next few years Sennacherib warred fiercely with Babylon. Finally, after a long siege, he conquered the city in 689 BCE. He razed it to the ground, along with Marduk's temple, and took the god's ritual statue to Assyria. His successor, Esarhaddon (680–669 BCE), rebuilt Babylon and brought Marduk's ritual image back to the city. Nevertheless, the relationship between Assyria and Babylonia remained difficult.

It was not until the late 7th century BCE, when the Assyrian Empire had lost its former strength, that Nabopolassar (625–605 BCE) succeeded in regaining Babylonia's independence. After almost two decades of conflict, Assyria was finally defeated, and Nabopolassar brought large parts of the former Assyrian territories under his control. This Neo-Babylonian Empire reached its pinnacle under his son Nebuchadnezzar II (604–562 BCE), stretching from the Mediterranean coast to the Zagros Mountains. Thus the city of Babylon experienced a second period of prosperity in the 7th and 6th centuries BCE, when exceptional monuments such as the Ishtar Gate and the Proces-

sional Way were built. But Babylon's return to supremacy did not last long. As early as 539 BCE, the Persian king Cyrus II (559–530 BCE) conquered the city, ending Babylonia's independence forever. Unlike the Babylonian rulers, the Persian kings left hardly any inscriptions documenting their construction activities. However, archaeological finds in Babylon indicate that many of the extant buildings were still in use in the Persian period.

Under the Macedonian king Alexander the Great (356–323 BCE), Babylon once again took on an important role. In 331 BCE, Alexander defeated the last Persian king, Darius III (336–330 BCE), in the Battle of Gaugamela, at the site of what is today Tell Gomel in northern Iraq. After this decisive victory, Alexander went to Babylon, where he entered the city without facing any resistance. The Babylonians immediately recognised him as king, and he used the traditional Mesopotamian royal title "king of the world" (*shar kishshati*). On the way back from his 10-year campaign, which took him as far as India, Alexander visited Babylon a second time, and he died there in the spring of 323 BCE. After his unexpected death, Alexander's generals waged several wars among themselves and eventually divided his vast empire. Babylon became part of the Seleucid Empire, named after the founder of the dynasty, Seleucus I.

Babylon retained its status as an important regional centre, both during the Seleucid period (320–141 BCE) and in the subsequent Parthian

Fig. 2: The Code of Hammurabi, king of Babylon (plaster copy VAG 131).

era (141 BCE–223 CE). Many Babylonian traditions endured under Persian, Greek, and Parthian rule. The temple rituals continued, especially in the sanctuary devoted to Marduk. These priests cultivated the culture of knowledge for which Babylon had been famous since Hammurabi's time. The so-called Babylonian Astronomical Diaries document this impressively. From around the 7th century BCE to the 1st century CE, these texts recorded astronomical observations as well as political and social events, such as Alexander's entrance into Babylon. The diaries also contain the last known references to the Ishtar Gate. In the year 126 BCE, the diaries recorded damage to a wall of blue-glazed bricks, and four years later they noted that the Ishtar Gate had suffered fire damage.[1] The most recent known clay tablet from Babylon dates to 74/75 CE. By that time, cuneiform writing had ceased to play a role in everyday life, and people had instead begun to use alphabetic scripts that were easier to learn.

From the 3rd century CE onwards, Babylon increasingly lost its importance, but it nevertheless remained populated. The so-called magic bowls – clay bowls with an Aramaic incantation carved on the inside, which date from the 5th to the 7th centuries CE – provide particular evidence of this, as do thousands of Sassanid and Islamic coins, the most recent of which dates to 819/820 CE. Furthermore, as late as the early 20th century, travellers reported encountering a village located in what would have been Babylon's urban area (see p. 40).

BABYLON UNDER NEBUCHADNEZZAR II

In the middle of the 1st millennium BCE, Babylon was one of the largest cities in the known world. Its extensive urban area covered about 950 hectares and provided living space for approximately 190,000 people.[2] Babylon would probably not seem very big to us today, since Berlin's Mitte district alone is about four times as big. To visitors at that time, however, it must have seemed huge. For comparison, ancient Athens was no more than 120 hectares in size, and approximately 40,000 people lived there.

But what did the city look like in Nebuchadnezzar II's time? We can imagine Babylon as a large construction site, with people digging foundations on every corner, transporting building materials, and raising walls, as well as making bricks on the outskirts of the city. There was a real construction boom in the 6th century BCE, and Nebuchadnezzar II erected many new monuments and large buildings, including the Ishtar Gate and the Processional Way. Mud bricks were traditionally utilized as a building material in Mesopotamia and continue to be used in the region today. They are inexpensive to produce and available in an almost unlimited supply, but without regular maintenance they do not last very long. Nebuchadnezzar II built most of his new buildings out of fired bricks. These were more durable, but producing them required large quantities of fuel, which was scarce on the alluvial plain around the Euphrates. Thus the city's wealth was evident at first sight. Moreover, the fired bricks have withstood the ages with less damage than the mud bricks, which is why Nebuchadnezzar II's city is the version of Babylon we know best today.

The city stretched along both banks of the Euphrates. Important official buildings, such as palaces and temples, were located on the eastern side of the river (Fig. 3). This part of the city was accessed via one of the five gates in the outer city wall, which Nebuchadnezzar II had built. The way into the centre of Babylon led through the extensive outer city, in the northern part of which was the king's so-called Summer Palace, located directly on the Euphrates. From the north, the colourful Processional Way and the Ishtar Gate led to the inner city, which was encompassed by another city wall. The street called *Ay-ibūr-shāpû* ("may the secret enemy not endure") continued from the Ishtar Gate past the temples of Ninmah and Ishtar. On the west side of the Euphrates, in the immediate vicinity of the Ishtar Gate, stood a huge palace complex facing the river, which the excavators called *Südburg* (Southern Palace). Adjacent to this was the temple district of Marduk, which constituted Babylon's religious centre. This district consisted of an extensive temple complex (*Etemenanki*) around the ziggurat, the biblical "Tower of Babel", as well as the sanctuary devoted to Marduk (*Esangil*). During the New Year festival, the most important religious event in Babylonia, the ceremonial procession wended its way along the route described above, down the Processional Way and through the Ishtar Gate to Marduk's temple (see pp. 30–31). The fact that the Ishtar Gate and the Processional Way were made of glazed bricks and decorated with symbols representing the gods clearly demonstrates the religious significance attached to them (see pp. 32–34). No other gate or street in Babylon was so elaborately embellished.

Immediately adjacent to the temples and the other official buildings was a residential quarter, to which the excavators gave the Arabic name *Merkes* (centre). The largest house they excavated, with a floor area of 1,900 square metres, seems more closely to approximate a stately residence than an ordinary dwelling. In these houses the excavators uncovered numerous clay tablet archives, which provide insights into the lives of Babylon's elite in the middle of the 1st millennium BCE. On the other hand, the residential areas where Babylon's "common people" lived have hardly been researched to date, and thus we know very little about their dwellings or their living conditions.

The same applies to the section of the city west of the Euphrates. This area has received very little archaeological attention, since the Euphrates runs further west today and large parts of the area have been flooded. In Nebuchadnezzar II's time, a bridge connected this part of the city to the rest, and it was also protected by a massive city wall. The western city was probably primarily an extensive residential area, where many families lived and worked. Additionally, according to a cuneiform text that describes the city of Babylon in detail, the district was divided into several quarters and included numerous temples.[3]

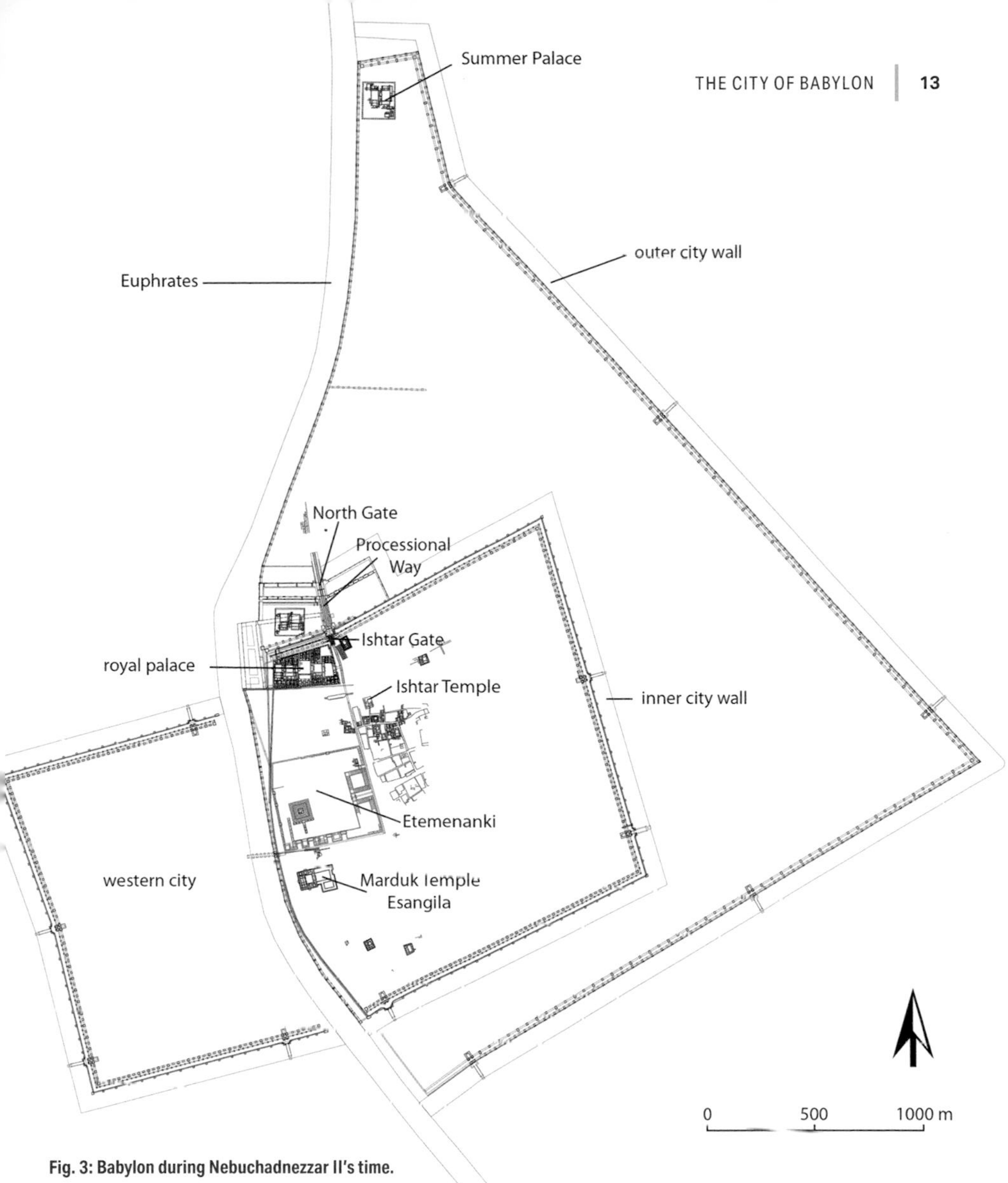

Summer Palace

outer city wall

Euphrates

North Gate

Processional Way

Ishtar Gate

royal palace

Ishtar Temple

inner city wall

Etemenanki

western city

Marduk Temple
Esangila

0   500   1000 m

Fig. 3: Babylon during Nebuchadnezzar II's time.

1 The two passages on the Ishtar Gate can be found in Abraham Sachs and Hermann Hunger (1996), *Astronomical Diaries and Related Texts from Babylonia, III: Diaries from 164 B.C. to 61 B.C.* (Vienna: Verl. der Österreichischen Akad. der Wiss.), No. -122A obv. 5-8 (1), -125A, obv. 14.

2 Calculating the number of inhabitants in ancient cities is problematic, as it depends on many, often unknown factors (open spaces, number of inhabitants per house etc.). An average value is 200 inhabitants per hectare, which is the calculation I used here.

3 The cuneiform text *Tintir* provides a description of the city of Babylon and its most important buildings. For a translation and commentary, see George 1992: 1–71.

Nebuchadnezzar II, King of Babylon

The Babylonian king Nebuchadnezzar II was not only responsible for constructing the Ishtar Gate and many other buildings in Babylon; he was also an extremely successful general. Under his leadership the Babylonian Empire reached its territorial zenith. Although today we primarily use the Hebrew form of his name, Nebuchadnezzar – which has been handed down in the Bible – his name in Babylonian is *Nabû-kudurrī-uṣur*, which roughly translates as: "Nabu, protect my son!" (Fig. 4). Nebuchadnezzar II was named after the glorious King Nebuchadnezzar I, who restored Babylonia's independence from Elam in the 12th century BCE (see p. 9).

Fig. 4: The so-called "Eye of Nebuchadnezzar" is probably a cast of an ancient eye stone. It depicts a warrior's head and includes a dedicatory inscription by Nebuchadnezzar II to the god Marduk (VA 1628).

Nebuchadnezzar II was born around 640 BCE, the son of King Nabopolassar (626–605 BCE). Nabopolassar had managed to break away from Assyrian suzerainty and had thus founded the Neo-Babylonian Empire. We know almost nothing about Nabopolassar's origins. In his inscriptions, he describes himself as "the son of no one", which suggests that he was not descended from an important Babylonian family. We also know relatively little about Nebuchadnezzar II himself or the political events of his reign, since no Neo-Babylonian state archives have yet been found. What we do know about Nebuchadnezzar II is mainly attested in his building inscriptions (Fig. 5). While these provide detailed information about his numerous construction projects, many other aspects of his life and times remain unexplored.

After first gaining dominion over Babylonia, Nabopolassar continued to expand his sphere of influence in subsequent years, bringing large parts of what was formerly Assyrian territory under his control. As crown prince, Nebuchadnezzar II had already successfully led military campaigns and won a decisive victory over Egypt in 605 BCE. The following year he succeeded his father to the throne and was crowned king of Babylon. The first years of his reign were marked by further campaigns to secure the territories in the western part of the empire permanently. In 597 BCE he conquered Jerusalem and carried the Judean king into captivity in Babylon. Ten years later he conquered Jerusalem a second time, destroyed the city, and deported a portion of the population. The Bible records this event, and the Judeans' deportation to Babylon has become known in collective memory as the Babylonian Exile. Nebuchadnezzar II's reign was extremely successful not only militarily, but also economically. One demonstration of this is his lively construction activity throughout Babylonia. His monuments and buildings permanently changed Babylon's cityscape (see pp. 11–13), and he also constructed and renovated buildings in other important Babylonian ritual centres, such as Borsippa near Babylon.

Nebuchadnezzar II had at least seven sons. When he died in 562 BCE, his son Amēl-Marduk succeeded him as king of Babylon. Amēl-Marduk took over a well-structured, prosperous empire, but he seems to have faced opposition from the very beginning of his reign. After only two years on the throne, his brother-in-law assassinated him.

The enduring impact of Nebuchadnezzar II's reign cannot be compared to that of any other ancient Near Eastern ruler. The Bible alone mentions him more than one hundred times. The Judeo-Christian tradition consistently portrays him negatively, as the destroyer of Jerusalem. In the Greek tradition, on the other hand, he is admired as a builder, and indeed Greek authors sometimes exaggerate his achievements (see pp. 38–39).

Fig. 5: Brick with a stamped cuneiform inscription: "Nebuchadnezzar [II], king of Babylon, the one who provides for Esangil and Ezida, the foremost heir of Nabopolassar, king of Babylon" (VA Bab 4060.03).

THE ISHTAR GATE AND THE PROCESSIONAL WAY

GLAZED BRICKS IN THE ANCIENT NEAR EAST

The brightly coloured Babylonian glazed bricks fascinated people even in ancient times and were known well beyond the borders of the Babylonian Empire. As the Persian king Darius I (522–486 BCE) wrote in the foundation charter for his palace in Susa (Iran):

The men who wrought the baked bricks, those were Babylonians.[4]

However, colour played an important role in Mesopotamian architecture long before the Babylonian Empire. As far back as the early Neolithic period, mud-brick walls were colourfully decorated, as demonstrated by the wall paintings in Tell Dscha'dat al-Mughara (present-day Syria) dating from the 9th millennium BCE. These colourful paintings provided a strong contrast to the beige-and-brown mud-brick architecture. With the development of glass and glaze production in the 2nd millennium BCE, a new technique became available – one which stood out from the traditional wall paintings due to its intense colours and singular radiance.

In the second half of the 2nd millennium BCE, in what is now south-western Iran, the Elamites first decorated buildings with coloured glazed bricks, knobs, and nails adorned with figures. From the 9th century BCE onwards, we have evidence of elaborate glazed brick panels in Assyria (present-day northern Iraq). These glazed paintings depict military campaigns, ritual scenes, and other small-scale representations similar to Assyrian palace reliefs (Fig. 6). In the 6th century BCE, under Nebuchadnezzar II, the Babylonians produced glazed bricks on a large scale for the first time. Compared to the older glazed bricks, these were distinguished by their bright blue colour. The Babylonians achieved this intense blue by adding cobalt ore, which was not yet in use when the Elamites and the Assyrians produced their earlier glazed bricks. The radiance of these glazes established the Babylonians' enduring reputation as skilled brickmakers. Glazed bricks continued to play an important role in the subsequent Persian period (550–330 BCE). Kings also elaborately decorated their palaces with glazed bricks during this period, as archaeological finds in Susa and Persepolis – as well as Babylon – prove. The glazed brick façades from the royal palace in Susa (Iran), some of which have been reconstructed and are now on display in the Louvre, are an impressive testament to the Persian ceramists' skill (Fig. 7). On the other hand, archaeologists have found only isolated evidence of glazed ornamentation used on buildings in the Hellenistic (332–140 BCE) and the Roman–Parthian periods (141 BCE–223 CE), as well as in the subsequent Sassanid era (224–632 CE). It was not until the early Islamic period that glazed ceramics were once again increasingly used in architecture. Such decoration remains a characteristic feature of Islamic architecture to this day.

The basic ingredients of glass and glazes – sand or quartz pebbles, plant ash, and lime – were easily accessible, but processing these materials required special technical knowledge. For example, a relatively high firing temperature of 900 to 1,100° C had to be reached and then maintained. Clay glazing was a particular challenge for craftsmen, since clay and glaze react differently to heat and expand and contract to different degrees in the firing process. This can easily create cracks in the clay or cause the glaze to flake off. Producing glazes in different colours required colouring agents such as copper oxide, cobalt, lead antimonates, and calcium antimonates, which do not naturally occur in Mesopotamia. These raw materials were probably sourced from various mines in the mountainous regions of present-day Turkey and Iran.

The labour-intensive process of producing glazed bricks involved many steps. First, the potters made the actual brick by spreading a prepared mixture of clay, sand, and finely chopped straw into a mould, letting the brick dry, and then firing it for the first time. The craftsmen assembled each relief animal used on the Ishtar Gate, the Processional Way, and the Throne Room Façade from various moulded bricks, each of which were made in a separate mould. A lion consisted of 46, a dragon of 40, and a bull of 44 different bricks.

Next the potters made marks on the top of each brick. These so-called fitters' marks in-

dicated the exact placement position for each brick so that it was possible to assemble the façade correctly at a later date without any problems. Then they applied the glazes, separating the individual colours with black glazed lines to prevent them from running together. After that, they had to fire the bricks a second time.

These glazed bricks, which required so much effort to produce, exclusively adorned

Fig. 6: An 8th-century BCE Assyrian glazed brick ortho-stat depicting a man praying before a deity (VA Ass 897).

Fig. 7: A reconstruction of Persian glazed bricks on display in the Louvre (Room 308). The original brick reliefs adorned King Darius I's palace in Susa (Iran) in the 6th/5th century BCE.

official buildings. In contrast to the much simpler wall paintings, glazes were far more robust, which is why the Mesopotamian kings mainly used them outdoors. Thus they decorated the courtyard façades of temples and palaces – or, as in the case of the Ishtar Gate, a ceremonial city gate and the splendid boulevard adjacent to it. The way these glazes shone in the sun's light seems to have been more important than their durability. According to the Mesopotamian aesthetic, differentiating the colours into individual shades was less of a priority than other properties, such as lustre and luminosity. It was precisely this aspect that Nebuchadnezzar II emphasised when he wrote that he had the Ishtar Gate built of "bricks (coloured with) shining blue glaze" (see pp. 24–26).

THE ISHTAR GATE

The Ishtar Gate was one of four city gates that provided access to Babylon's inner city. It constituted the entrance to the city's ritual and political centre, where the temple of the city god Marduk, the sanctuaries of other important deities, and the palace were located. Like the other gates in the inner city wall, it is named after a deity: Ishtar, the goddess of war and sexuality (see p. 27). The Babylonian name of the gate was *Ishtar-sākipat-tēbîsha*: "Ishtar repels its attacker". Taken as a whole, the city walls were the largest structure in Babylon in the Neo-Babylonian period (626–539 BCE). Nabopolassar, Nebuchadnezzar II's father, had already begun to extend the city's defences. His son continued these efforts by adding the

7.5 kilometre-long outer city wall and signifi-cantly strengthening the inner city fortifica-tions, which then consisted of a double wall that was approximately 40 metres wide, with an embankment of fired bricks fronted by a moat. The city gates were all designed in the same way: each was made up of two gates, with the smaller front gate leading through the outer cir-cular wall and the main gate through the inner circular wall. The entire passage through both gates was between 50 and 54 metres long. The protrusions next to the passages emphasised the enormity of these structures. According to pictorial representations, these were topped to look like towers, which added to the overall impression of a fortress. The only difference be-tween the Ishtar Gate and the other gates was its rich decoration. The reconstruction in the *Vorderasiatisches Museum* displays only one

side of the smaller front gate from the original double-gate structure.

Restoring the city's fortifications was an enormous construction project that required immense resources. It is all the more aston-ishing that Nebuchadnezzar II had the Ishtar Gate restored three times in the course of his 43-year reign. Each of these three gates stood directly on the walls of the previous structure. Due to the construction of the new royal palace, the so-called Southern Palace, the level of the surrounding area had risen so much that the streets and subsequently also the gates had to be raised as well; this procedure is characteris-tic of mud-brick settlements. After removing all the building materials that could be reused, the workers involved in the new construction par-tially tore down the masonry of the older build-ings, filled the remains with rubble, and levelled

Fig. 0: The remains of the Ishtar Gate's earliest construction phase, which still stand in Babylon today.

the surface. After this preparation process, they placed the new building on top of the previous masonry. In this way, settlement layers continued to rise over time.

In all three of its construction phases, the Ishtar Gate depicted two divine symbolic animals: *Mušhuššu* the snake-dragon represented the city god, Marduk, while the bull embodied the weather god, Adad (see pp. 32–34). The construction phases differed in their execution, however. The oldest gate consisted of unglazed, sculpted bricks with relief depictions. This phase has been preserved in Babylon and still stands today, reaching a height of 15 to 18 metres. The excavation team uncovered up to nine rows of animals, arranged one atop the other – always alternating between a row of bulls and a row of dragons. Visitors can still see the impressive remains of this monument onsite in Babylon today (Fig. 8). The excavators discovered only small remains of the second construction phase. Up to 20 layers of flat, colourfully glazed bricks

still stood directly atop the older gate structure. These depicted the lower part of a bull, a row of rosettes, and a black-and-yellow geometric decorative band (Fig. 9). Further fragments of these flat glazed bricks prove that they depicted not only bulls, but also dragons in this construction phase (Fig. 11).

No upright walls from the gate structure's third, most recent construction phase had survived in Babylon – there was only glazed brick fragments. The museum team later reconstructed the gate's third construction phase from a combination of original fragments and modern bricks in the *Vorderasiatisches Museum*, modelling it on the earlier construction phases (Fig. 10).

Why have only fragments from the third construction phase survived? In all three construction phases, Nebuchadnezzar II had the entire gate structure built from durable fired bricks and not, as was otherwise customary, from air-dried mud bricks. In fact, this solid building ma-

terial is the reason for the Ishtar Gate's poor state of preservation, because people in antiquity had already begun to remove the ruins in order to reuse the robust fired bricks from the structure's interior as building material. They could not put the glazed bricks to use, however, which is why most of them remained onsite. When Robert Koldewey came to Babylon in search of a suitable excavation site, he immediately noticed these glazed brick fragments. His team systematically searched the rubble and collected even the inconspicuous glazed brick fragments. Based on these pieces, the excavators painstakingly reconstructed the animals representing the gods as well as the ornamental motifs on the Ishtar Gate – first on the drawing board, and later in the museum (see pp. 56–61).

The earlier construction phases, which were still in place, formed the basis for the reconstruction: a row of bulls was followed in turn by a row of dragons, and so forth. The fragments found in Babylon prove that each of the two animals originally existed in two versions: one in whitish-beige and one in yellowish-orange. The curly fur on the wild bull's belly and back was turquoise. If both the front and the main gate were covered with animals in relief, then there must have originally been at least 557 animals. Based on the numerous blue fragments found in this area, the excavators also presumed that blue-glazed bricks had covered the entire gate. However, archaeologists are uncertain whether the battlements were constructed of glazed bricks, as they are

Fig. 9: The remains of the Ishtar Gate's two older construction phases at the time the excavation began, Babylon 1902.

Fig. 10: The reconstruction of the Ishtar Gate's most recent construction phase, displayed in the Pergamon Museum.

Fig. 11: The gate's second construction phase, reconstructed from small fragments in the *Vorderasiatisches Museum*.

in the museum reconstruction. Babylonian representations usually depict triangular battlements, but no glazed bricks in this shape were found. Even if the production of glazed bricks was highly standardised and all the relief bricks of a particular type were made from identical moulds, the production of so many glazed bricks must nevertheless have been a technical and logistical challenge, even in the flourishing Neo-Babylonian Empire.

The visibility of the animals representing the gods increased each time the gate structure was refurbished. In the earliest construction phase, for example, the dragon and the bull – which were made of unglazed relief bricks – were only visible when the light was favourable. The depictions of these animals on the flat, glazed bricks of the second phase were already much more visible. The Ishtar Gate developed its full effect in the final phase, when Nebuchadnezzar II combined relief bricks with brightly coloured glazes. In Babylon's characteristically brilliant sunlight, this must have presented an impressive play of colours, which would have been further enlivened by the reflections on the sculpted surfaces.

"TO BE AN OBJECT OF WONDER FOR ALL THE PEOPLE, I FILLED THOSE GATES WITH SPLENDOUR" – THE INSCRIPTION ON THE ISHTAR GATE

In the process of excavating in Babylon, the excavators found numerous fragments depicting white-glazed cuneiform signs on a blue background. These were part of an inscription that was once attached to the Ishtar Gate. Furthermore, the different sizes of the cuneiform signs indicate several inscriptions. However, scholars have been unable to deduce the content of the inscriptions from these small pieces of brick, as the preserved remains are too fragmented.

For this reason, efforts to reconstruct the inscription were initially dispensed with during the reconstruction of the Ishtar Gate in the Pergamon Museum. In May 1931, less than a year after the Pergamon Museum opened, the conservators finally assembled a sixty-line inscription from the brick fragments and subsequently inserted it on the left-hand side of the gate (Fig. 13). Since the excavators in Babylon had discovered most of the bricks depicting cuneiform signs in the same area, it is likely that Nebuchadnezzar had indeed placed an inscription here. However, because the fragments were incomplete, the conservators had to supplement the inscription extensively, and many of the cuneiform characters were constructed from scratch.

Nebuchadnezzar II's longest known inscription, the so-called East India House Inscription, served as a model for the reconstructed inscription. This inscription survived on a stone tablet, which was discovered in Babylon prior to 1803 by the British diplomat Harford Jones-Brydges, who was working for the East India Company. This tablet has been in the British Museum in London since 1938 (Fig. 12). The text describes the construction of the Northern Palace, but it also contains passages on other building projects in Babylon. With regard to the Ishtar Gate, it says:

Fig. 12: The so-called East India House Inscription, including Nebuchadnezzar II's report on the construction of the Ishtar Gate.

Fig. 13: The reconstructed, newly supplemented inscription on the Ishtar Gate in Berlin (VA Bab 7661).

(As for) *Ishtar-sākipat-tēbîsha* [= the Babylonian name of the Ishtar Gate], both gates of *Imgur-Enlil* and *Nēmetti-Enlil* [the names of the two masons who built the inner city wall], their entrances became too low as a result of the raising (of the level) of the street of Babylon [= the Processional Way]. I removed those gates and (then) secured their foundation(s) at the level of the water table with bitumen and fired brick. I had (them) skilfully built with fired bricks (coloured with) shining blue glaze that have (representations of) wild bulls (and) *Mušḫuššu*-dragon(s) fashioned upon them (lit. "it"). I had (beams of) hard cedar stretched (over them) as their roofs. At each of its gates, I hung doors (made) of cedar with a facing of bronze (and) threshold(s) and fittings of cast copper. At their door-jambs I stationed fierce wild bulls of copper and raging *Mušḫuššu*-dragons. To

be an object of wonder for all the people, I filled those gates with splendour.[5]

Babylonian building inscriptions always ended with the naming of the building for which they were made. The reconstructed inscription in Berlin includes Nebuchadnezzar II's official titles and the passage on the Ishtar Gate, as well as a concluding section on the New Year Festival House. In its modern form, therefore, it cannot correspond to the one on the original Ishtar Gate. Moreover, building inscriptions were not normally visible, but rather hidden inside the masonry. They informed subsequent builders about the original builder and honoured his deeds. We do not know whether the inscriptions on the Ishtar Gate were comparable texts, as they were visibly mounted on the gate and no corresponding inscriptions are known to us.

THE PROCESSIONAL WAY OF BABYLON

The very name Processional Way already indicates its function. On this road, during the annual New Year festival, the procession of the gods moved from the New Year Festival House outside the city back into the city centre, and finally to Marduk's temple. We find the following inscription written on stone paving slabs (Fig. 14):

Nebuchadnezzar [II], king of Babylon, son of Nabopolassar, king of Babylon, am I. (As for) the street of Babylon (*Ay-ibūr-shābū*), for the processional street of the great lord, the god Marduk, I beautified (its) access way with slab(s) of breccia. O Marduk, my lord, grant me a long life![6]

The inscription informs us not only about the king who built the street, but also about its name and its purpose. According to this information, the street was conducive to the procession, and thus the modern name Processional Way reflects its original function. It is also called the "street of Babylon", a name which emphasises its special significance. The street's Babylonian name is *Ay-ibūr-shāpû*, which means "may the secret enemy not endure". The Processional Way also

Fig. 14: A fragment of a stone paving slab from the Processional Way, with an inscription by Nebuchadnezzar II (VA Bab 4500).

Who Was the Goddess Ishtar?

Fig. 15: The goddess Ishtar with a lion, depicted on a cylinder seal from the 3rd millennium BCE. The weapons underline the goddess's martial nature (VA 3605).

Ishtar is one of the seven main deities and the most important goddess in the Mesopotamian pantheon. She is the goddess of war and sexuality, although her martial aspect dominates her character. She was also identified with the planet Venus, the morning and evening star. Ishtar was thus one of the most multi-faceted and also one of the most eccentric deities in ancient Mesopotamia. Her spirited, capricious, and quick-tempered nature was the subject of numerous myths. In the eponymous epic, Gilgamesh incurred the goddess' wrath when he rejected her advances, referring to the unpleasant fate of her former lovers. Surviving narratives mostly describe her as young, unmarried, and childless. Pictorial representations often depict Ishtar as a warrior goddess with weapons protruding from her shoulders (Fig. 15). The lion – the epitome of strength, power, and danger – is her companion animal and underlines her martial nature. Depictions often show Ishtar standing on the backs of lions, in a chariot drawn by lions, or sitting on a lion throne. A lion depicted alone could also represent the goddess, as it does on the Processional Way (see p. 30). She is most often represented by an eight-pointed star, as the embodiment of the so-called Star of Venus.

The goddess Ishtar is one of the earliest Mesopotamian deities we can identify by means of archaeological finds. Her cult can be traced back to the 4th millennium BCE, in Uruk in southern Iraq. From the middle of the 3rd millennium BCE, she is attested there under her Sumerian name, Inana, which translates as "Lady of Heaven". Today she is mostly known to us under the Semitic variant of her name, as Ishtar. Ishtar was widely worshipped throughout Mesopotamia. Shrines to her are attested in Uruk and numerous other sites in present-day Iraq and Syria. She played an important role in the royal cult as defender of the land and protector of the troops. The general population also highly venerated Ishtar, as evidenced by numerous less-valuable gifts presented to the goddess, which have been discovered at her shrines and are represented on cylinder seals.

bore another name: "Ishtar is the patron goddess of her army" (*Ishtar-lamassi-ummānīshu*).[7] This seems to refer to the area in the immediate vicinity of the gate. The various names of the Processional Way and the Ishtar Gate underline their importance in Babylonian cultic proceedings.

The area outside the city centre to the north of the Ishtar Gate was decorated with glazed relief animals similar to those on the gate itself. The people who participated in the procession were met with lions – the goddess Ishtar's representative animal – with their mouths wide open. After passing through the Ishtar Gate, the Processional Way continued south along the palace wall to Marduk's temple, but this part of the street was not decorated with the elaborate glazed bricks. The excavators were able to follow the course of this street for a length of 1.2 kilometres. The stone pavement was still present in places. Stonemasons had inscribed the edges of many of the paving slabs in such a way that the inscription could not be seen once they were laid (see p. 26).

Nebuchadnezzar II was probably responsible for extending the Processional Way north of the Ishtar Gate. This part of the street was no longer located in Babylon's traditional inner city area, but it was within the outer wall Nebuchadnezzar II had completed. The king created an open square directly in front of the Ishtar Gate. This was probably where the New Year celebrations took place before the procession passed through the gate and entered Babylon's inner city. Nebuchadnezzar II built two other

Fig. 16: A model of the Ishtar Gate, the Processional Way, and the North Gate, which was discovered later.

Fig. 17: The reconstruction of the Processional Way in the Pergamon Museum.

structures that bordered the Processional Way, which was 20–24 metres wide: to the west, the so-called Northern Palace, an extension of the royal palace; and to the east, the so-called Eastern Outwork, a massive fortification in front of the inner city wall. The walls of these fortifications, articulated with projections and recesses, enclosed the street along a length of 190 metres. During Iraqi excavations in 1981, archaeologists discovered the North Gate, which Nebuchadnezzar II also built and which constituted the northern end of the Processional Way (Fig. 16).[8]

As with the Ishtar Gate, we can trace evidence of several construction phases for the Processional Way, and here too the street level was raised several times. It seems that only the final phase included lions as representative decoration. At the very least, archaeologists have discovered no unglazed lion reliefs or depictions of lions on flat bricks, as they found in the Ishtar Gate's earlier construction phases. The use of glazed relief animals as decoration is likely to have been contemporary with the gate's final construction phase. Here again, no standing walls had survived, but excavators found thousands of fragments of lion reliefs in the area north of the gate. They also excavated the remains of the older walls of the so-called Northern Palace and the Eastern Outwork. As was the case with the Ishtar Gate and the other monumental buildings constructed under Nebuchadnezzar II, people had also removed these walls at various points up to the modern period so that they could reuse the bricks; by the time the excavation took place, the road was at a higher level than the boundary walls. Over a length of about 180 metres, approximately 120 lions must have adorned the surrounding walls – 60 on each side.

Each lion was made up of 46 different relief bricks stacked atop each other in 11 rows. The lions' mouths were wide open and their tails were lowered, in contrast to the lions on the Throne Room Façade. In terms of colour, the lions came in two different versions: one group had whitish-beige coats and luxuriant orange manes and tail tassels, while the other group had orange coats and greenish manes. The background against which the lions stood was either vibrant blue or bright turquoise. Fragments of whitish-yellow rosettes and decorative bands in yellow, black, and white complemented these figurative representations. The walls of

Festivals and Processions

The fact that the Ishtar Gate and the Processional Way were elaborately decorated with animals representing the gods – lions, dragons, and bulls – clearly shows that they held religious significance beyond their everyday functions as a gate and a street (see pp. 32–34). Together they constituted the ritual entrance to the inner city, leading to the temples of the deities Ninmah, Ishtar, Nabu, and Marduk, who was both the city god of Babylon and the most important god in the entire Babylonian Empire (Fig. 18).

The Ishtar Gate and the Processional Way played a special role in the *akītu* festival, the Babylonian New Year festival. This eleven-day celebration always took place in the spring and was the most important religious event of the year, when the Babylonians invoked divine blessings for the land's fertility and the state's prosperity. In addition, the gods confirmed the reigning king in his official role at the New Year festival, thus (re)legitimising royal rule every year. Thanks to cuneiform texts commissioned by the Babylonian kings, we can establish the course of these celebrations fairly precisely.

Every year at the New Year festival, all the gods of the whole country gathered in Babylon; their ritual images travelled in large processions from various cities across Babylonia. The festivities first honoured the chief Babylonian god, Marduk, in his sanctuary, known as *Esangil*. Over the course of the festival, the king courted the favour of his "lord Marduk", who ultimately ritually crowned the king. The first meeting between the god and the king took place on the fifth day of the festivities. On the ninth day, Marduk and the "gods of heaven and earth", accompanied by the king, processed from Marduk's temple to the New Year Festival House (*akītu* house) outside the city – the exact location of which is still unknown today. The route that the statues of the gods and the participants in the procession took from the city centre to the Festival House probably also included travel by boat on the Euphrates for part of the way. On the way back to the city on the eleventh and final day of the New Year festival, the gods and the ceremonial procession took the route along the Processional Way and through the Ishtar Gate, back to the temple of Marduk.

Fig. 18: The god Marduk with the snake-dragon *Mušhuššu* on a Babylonian cylinder seal (VA Bab 646).

How can we picture these processions? The king and the ritual image of the god Marduk were positioned at the head of the procession, followed by numerous other statues of deities. The wooden figures of the gods were dressed in precious robes and sat on their richly decorated thrones. They were accompanied by priests – who prayed, played music, and waved incense – as well as the people of Babylon. Unfortunately no pictorial representations have survived, but it is easy to imagine that the procession was a spectacular sight as it passed along the Processional Way and through the Ishtar Gate, with the brightly coloured glazed bricks dazzling in the sunlight.

the surrounding buildings, which were certainly quite high, were quite probably not completely covered with glazed bricks, but were rather plastered above the lions, similarly to how they appear in the *Vorderasiatisches Museum*. Due to the poor state of preservation, the question of whether the blue glazed-brick battlements reproduced in the museum were also part of the original must remain open (Fig. 17).

The Processional Way recreated in the museum is much shorter and narrower than it once was in Babylon. For example, in Berlin there are only 12 lions on each side. Moreover, the Processional Way was originally about three times as wide as the modern reconstruction in the museum – at a width of 20–24 metres. Apart from these features, however, the reconstruction is strongly oriented towards the findings in Babylon. Just as people would have done 2,600 years ago, the visitor walks along the Processional Way, which is structured with projections and recesses, towards the Ishtar Gate.

THE GODS' ANIMAL REPRESENTATIVES: LION, DRAGON, AND BULL

The lion, the dragon, and the bull on the Ishtar Gate and the Processional Way are not merely decoration; they represent three of the most important Babylonian gods. The lion represents Ishtar; the bull – or more precisely, the wild bull – embodies the weather god, Adad; and the dragon symbolises Marduk, the city god of Babylon. With Babylon's rise from a city-state to a great kingdom, Marduk became the supreme god of all Babylonia, presiding over the other gods as their king. He also played an important political role, legitimising the mortal king's rule over Babylonia by confirming him in his official role at the New Year festival every year (see pp. 30–31).

Beginning in the 3rd millennium BCE, animals or supernatural creatures often represented the gods in Mesopotamia. These instantiations of the gods referred to the deity's character. Weapons usually stood for martial deities;

Fig. 19: A reconstructed lion with a turquoise mane on the Processional Way.

Fig. 20: The bull representing the weather god on the Ishtar Gate.

the stylus and the clay tablet signified the god of scribes, Nabu; while the lamp symbolised the god of light, Nusku. Ishtar and Adad were both represented by natural animals known for their characteristic strength and ferocity. The lion symbolised Ishtar's martial character (Fig. 19), while the wild bull stood for the weather god's unbridled temperament (Fig. 20). The supreme god Marduk, on the other hand, was embodied by a hybrid, dragon-like creature that combined various elements. This creature had the head of a snake, the forelegs of a lion, the hind legs of a bird of prey, and a scorpion's sting on its long tail (Fig. 21). Thanks to Nebuchadnezzar II's inscription for the Ishtar Gate, we also know this creature's name – *Mušhuššu*, which means "fearsome serpent" (see pp. 24–26).

In addition to these animals, stylised rosettes also adorned both the Ishtar Gate and the Processional Way, as well as the so-called Throne Room Façade. This led scholars to consider whether the rosette might also be a symbol for the goddess Ishtar. The rosette had been a frequent motif in ancient Near Eastern art since the 5th millennium BCE and generally seems to have been imbued with positive meaning. In addition to buildings, it was also used to adorn garments, jewellery, weapons, and various kinds of vessels. While scholars have not been able to establish any direct reference to the goddess, the rosettes were presumably intended to provide additional protection for the gate.

At first, it may seem surprising that the animals representing the gods Marduk and Adad (the dragon and the bull, respectively) were placed on the Ishtar Gate, but not the lion – Ishtar's representative animal. These animals not only represented the gods, but could also figuratively ward off disaster. Gates were places of transition, and at the same time they were weak points in the walls. Therefore they required special protection. For this purpose,

Fig. 21: The snake-dragon *Mušhuššu* on the Ishtar Gate.

from the 3rd millennium BCE onwards, images of lions, bulls, and dragons were positioned at gates. Thus the animals representing the gods on the Ishtar Gate and the Processional Way not only symbolised three important deities, but also protected the gate, and with it the entire city. The desire to repel intruders is also expressed in the Babylonian names of the Ishtar Gate ("Ishtar repels its attacker") and the Processional Way ("may the secret enemy not endure").

Since the Ishtar Gate, as the gate leading to the inner city, had less a defensive than a symbolic significance, surely the reference here is not only to military attacks, but also to political opponents or rebels from within the city itself. Thus the Ishtar Gate and the Processional Way were not simply a gate, a street, and a religious monument, but also an exhortation to respect the will of the gods, and thus that of the king as well.

---

4   A thorough commentary on and translation of Darius I's inscription can be found in Roland G. Kent (1953), *Old Persian. Grammar, Texts, Lexicon* (New Haven: American Oriental Society), p. 144 § 3 k.

5   For a complete translation of the reconstructed inscription on the Ishtar Gate (No. 101), as well as the India House Inscription (No. 2), see http://oracc.museum.upenn.edu/ribo/babylon7/corpus (accessed 28 Oct. 2021). Information on the structure of both the reconstructed and the original inscriptions can be found in Pedersén 2020: 116–117.

6   Translated with reference to http://oracc.org/ribo/Q005478/ (accessed 28 Oct. 2021).

7   The various street names have survived in the cuneiform text *Tintir* (see n. 3 above). For translations and locations of the streets, see Pedersén 2020: 201–204, with further references.

8   Since the North Gate was only discovered in 1981, it is missing from most maps and also from the model of the Processional Way and the Ishtar Gate in the Pergamon Museum.

THE THRONE ROOM FAÇADE AT NEBUCHADNEZZAR II'S PALACE

Nebuchadnezzar II lavishly decorated his palace with glazed bricks as well. While the Ishtar Gate and the Processional Way played an important role in religious festivals, the king placed the so-called Throne Room Façade inside the palace, and thus it was only visible to a very exclusive circle of people. It adorned the main courtyard of the royal palace of Babylon (Southern Palace). Nebuchadnezzar II had the huge palace complex completely rebuilt. With almost 600 rooms as well as five large and approximately 50 smaller courtyards, it was the largest building in Babylon. The throne room adjoined the central main courtyard, and Nebuchadnezzar II decorated its 56-metre-long courtyard façade with

glazed bricks (Fig. 22). Mesopotamian rulers often decorated precisely this courtyard façade in their palaces particularly richly, but we do not know of any comparable façade decoration from any other palace.

As with the Ishtar Gate, the walls on which Nebuchadnezzar II placed the Throne Room Façade were no longer standing at the time of the excavation, and only fragments of the glazed brick decoration in the main courtyard of the palace have survived. However, the excavators found one fallen piece of the glazed brick façade about seven metres from the former courtyard façade. Although the bricks were broken, they were still in their original context, with

Fig. 22: Reconstruction showing how the Throne Room Façade in Babylon's royal palace may have looked. Painting by Elisabeth Andrae (VAK 20).

Fig. 23: Drawing of the section of the Throne Room Façade that was found in one piece. Watercolour by Walter Andrae, 1901 (ArDOG V.28.18).

the glazes facing downwards, and thus provided an initial clue for the reconstruction of the motifs (Fig. 23). Based on this sample, the Throne Room Façade depicted a completely different spectrum of images than the Ishtar Gate and the Processional Way. In the palace, the excavators primarily found highly stylised floral representations – such as palm tree trunks crowned with volute capitals, flower garlands, ornamental bands decorated with palmettes, and bands of rosettes. These recurring motifs were executed in orange, white, black, and turquoise on a bright blue background. The colours contrasted sharply with the brownish-grey mud-brick architecture. This may have been intended to give the impression of a garden with palm trees, lush flowers, and waterways.

In addition, the excavators found many fragments of sculpted lions in the Southern Palace. These resembled the lions on the Processional Way, with the exception of one detail: while the lions along the Processional Way always appeared with their tails lowered, the lions in the palace carried their tails high. They also found lion fragments in other areas in addition to the main courtyard of the palace, which is why we can assume that these lions were also used to decorate other courtyards. Koldewey reconstructed the

lions in a frieze under the floral representations on the Throne Room Façade, so that the animals approached each other from both sides of the courtyard. The excavation in the main courtyard, however, offered no evidence for such an arrangement of the motifs, one above the other. In spite of the fragmentary state of preservation and the lack of parallels, various scholars have proposed other reconstructions that are also worth considering. These differ primarily in terms of the division of the walls, the distribution of the ornaments, and the design of the palmette trees.

The two sections of the Throne Room Façade that Walter Andrae reconstructed in the Pergamon Museum consist almost exclusively of modern bricks. Only the lions and the lower decorative bands are partly composed of original brick fragments (Fig. 24). By contrast, the upper sections, with their stylised palms and floral ornaments, are made entirely of modern bricks. The arrangement of the motifs deviates from the excavators' original reconstructions because it had to be adapted to the museum space. In addition, the Throne Room Façade is not shown as a whole, but rather in two separate sections on either side of the Ishtar Gate. Due to the situation at the excavation site (as described above), this reconstruction remains hypothetical.

Fig. 24: Reconstruction of the Throne Room Façade in the *Vorderasiatisches Museum*.
The entire upper area is made of modern bricks (VA Bab 1457–1482).

EXPLORING BABYLON

BETWEEN TRUTH AND EXAGGERATION – CLASSICAL SOURCES ON BABYLON

Archaeological research on Babylon only began in the 19th century. Nevertheless, Babylon has never been completely forgotten; it is firmly anchored in Christian–Jewish thought, and it also plays a role in the Islamic tradition (see pp. 68–70). In addition to the biblical tradition, Greek and Roman authors were primarily responsible for maintaining knowledge of the ancient city in Europe.

The best-known and most influential work on Mesopotamia in classical antiquity is Herodotus's *Histories*, written in the 5th century BCE and completely preserved. For centuries, readers understood Herodotus's text as a purely factual account, and therefore researchers attempted to reconcile any discovery in Babylon with his descriptions. Today we know that this work mixes history with stories; events that were directly observed are placed alongside hearsay. As a whole, the work ultimately served Herodotus's stated aim: that "the memory of the past may not be blotted out from among men by time".[9] Neither the excavated archaeological remains nor the customs described in cuneiform texts match his descriptions. Yet scholars continued to view Babylon through this "Herodotian filter" until well into the 20th century. More recent research takes a more critical view, but the image Herodotus created continues to exert a subliminal influence on our collective imagination.

A detailed account of Babylon is also found in Ctesias's *Persica*, written in the early 4th century BCE and only partly preserved. Ctesias was a Greek physician in the service of the Persian king. Like Herodotus, most of Ctesias's descriptions do not correspond to archaeological findings. However, he chronicled walls of coloured bricks with animals carved on them, which inevitably calls to mind the glazed bricks of the Ishtar Gate, the Processional Way, and the Throne Room Façade.[10] Ctesias combined what was known from other works with his own observations and also with rumours. He embellished his stories to correspond to his contemporaries' expectations. The picture he painted of "oriental" splendour and decadence is based on oriental clichés that are still common today: effeminate despots, harem culture, and dissolute luxury.

Another source of which only excerpts survive is the historical work of Berossos in Greek. Berossos, a contemporary of Alexander the Great, was a priest of Marduk in Babylon. Since he had access to cuneiform texts, he had an intimate knowledge of Babylonian life and culture that no other Greek possessed. The few passages that have come down to us align quite well with older native sources. His descriptions of Babylon's buildings largely correspond to the so-called East India House Inscription (see p. 25). The only exception is the famous Hang-

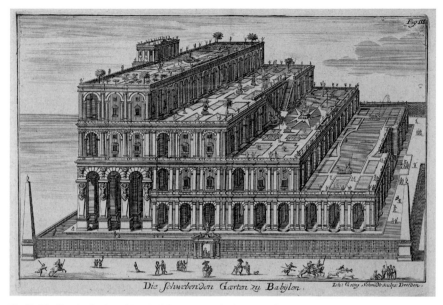

Fig. 25: "The Hanging Gardens of Babylon". Copper engraving by Johann Georg Schmidt (1694–1767).

ing Gardens, which he mentioned for the first time and to which the cuneiform texts make no reference.[11] In fact, these gardens may not have existed in Babylon at all. Numerous classical authors also described hanging gardens from the 2nd century BCE onwards, but there is no consensus on who built them (Fig. 25).[12]

According to classical sources, Babylon fell into decay beginning in the 3rd century BCE.[13] Thus the Roman historian Cassius Dio writes that the emperor Trajan (53–117 CE) was disappointed during his visit to Babylon in 116 CE because all that remained of the famous city were "mounds and stones and ruins". Archaeological finds, on the other hand, suggest that the Babylonian temples and the settlement itself lasted until the 4th century CE, albeit on a smaller scale than previously (see p. 11).

TRAVELLERS, ADVENTURERS, AND THE FIRST ARCHAEOLOGISTS

As early as the Roman era, a sea of ruins was all that was left to remind the visitor of the former metropolis – and yet knowledge of Babylon was never completely lost. The Babylonians originally built the city primarily with Mesopotamia's characteristic air-dried mud bricks. Without regular renewal and maintenance, mud-brick buildings will decay almost completely within 50 to 70 years. Thus the local population was primarily responsible for preserving Babylon's memory and maintaining knowledge of the site's exact location. To this day, the Babylonian name of the city, *Bābili* ("Gate of the God") lives on in the Arabic name *Bābil* (see pp. 68–70). The population of the surrounding towns and villages sustained an awareness of ancient Babylon primarily thanks to the fact that they reused the bricks from the former metropolis. In order to do so, over the centuries they removed the remains of the old buildings down to the foundations. This was a common practice until the early 20th century, and travellers repeatedly reported seeing "brick robbers" in Babylon.

The early Islamic travellers and chroniclers Al-Istakhrī (الإصطخري) and Ibn Hawqal (ابن حوقل) mentioned Babylon in the 9th and 10th centuries CE. The former had probably visited Babylon himself, whereas Ibn Hawqal was most likely drawing on the work Al-Istakhrī, who was his teacher. Both men referred to Babylon as "the oldest place in the land". Other Islamic scholars in the 9th to the 14th centuries CE, such as the famous geographer al-Idrīsī (الإدريسي), pointed out that only a small village remained on the site. It seems that the ruins of the ancient city were clearly visible at that time. Archaeological finds from later excavations prove that Babylon was populated during this period, albeit on a much smaller scale than during its heyday, in the middle of the 1st millennium BCE (see p. 11). Apart from personal observations made on site, scholars of the Islamic world – as well as Europeans – had only the Greek and Roman sources at their disposal (see above), because scribes proficient in cuneiform had disappeared by the beginning in the 1st century CE.

The first Europeans were drawn to Babylon from the Middle Ages onwards. As early as the 12th century, the Jewish travellers Benjamin of Tudela and Petachiah of Regensburg visited Mesopotamia, and probably Babylon as well (Fig. 26). Since their travel reports appeared much later and in an abridged form, it is not possible to distinguish with any certainty between what they actually saw and what they merely heard about. However, their reports are an early testimony to the European interest in the biblical sites.

In the subsequent centuries, European travellers – including notable explorers such as Marco Polo (1254–1324) – made isolated reports on Babylon. Like subsequent travellers, Marco Polo tried to reconcile what he found with ancient and biblical traditions. While local traditions maintained a knowledge of where Babylon was, travellers from Europe occasionally got confused. Foreigners often mistook the striking ruins of the ancient stepped temples – called Ziggurrat – in Birs Nimrud (ancient Borsippa) in Babylon's immediate vicinity and in Aqar Quf (ancient Dūr Kurigalzu) near Baghdad for the biblical Tower of Babylon/Babel. In addition, travellers equated Baghdad with Babylon to some extent, and they had a tendency to identify Aqar Quf as ancient Babylon. We must therefore evaluate the medieval reports written by Europeans with particular caution in terms of their authenticity and truthfulness. Many travellers were on the road as traders or pilgrims, so their texts primarily reflect the author's personal views – over which biblical tradition exerted a strong influence – and have no claim to be academic.

Only in the 16th century did the number of reports about Mesopotamia and its ancient sites increase considerably, as did their level of detail. It was at this time that travellers brought the first antiquities from Babylon to Europe. The first realistic description of the site came from the Italian nobleman and explorer Pietro della Valle (1586–1652). He correctly identified Babylon and recognised the connection between the Arabic *Bābil* and the accounts of Babel handed down in the Bible. In addition, he was the first to copy cuneiform texts and to carry out excavations in Mesopotamia. Although della Valle's reports were widely circulated and many later travellers and explorers referred to him, they continued to confuse Babylon with Borsippa and Aqar Quf until the 19th century.

Babylon was also very popular with European travellers in the 18th and 19th centuries. Many explorers brought their finds back to Europe, including such important pieces as the East India House Inscription (see p. 25). Carsten Niebuhr (1733–1815), a German explorer in the service of the Danish king, made sketches of the site and measured it for the first time. The French cleric and astronomer Pierre Joseph de Beauchamp (1752–1801) visited the ruins of Babylon in the 1780s, where he observed local farmers digging for bricks who found "a cow, the sun, and the moon depicted on glazed bricks".[14] The cow made of glazed bricks must have been one of the bulls from the Ishtar Gate. Thus de Beauchamp provided the first direct reference to the Ishtar Gate since antiquity.

Archaeological research in Babylon began with the British traveller Claudius James Rich (1787–1821), who made the first detailed map of the ruins in 1811, carried out small excavations, and published the results. Rich was the East India Company's resident in Baghdad at the time. He was quite gifted in languages, mastering various ancient and modern languages of the region, and was interested in antiquity. British travellers were also drawn to Babylon in subsequent years: in 1850, Austen

Fig. 26: A 19th-century engraving of Benjamin of Tudela.

Henry Layard (1817–1894) excavated there and sent some of his finds to the British Museum, including glazed bricks from the Ishtar Gate. After only a short time, however, Layard – the pioneer of "archaeology" in Mesopotamia and excavator of the Assyrian royal cities of Nineveh and Nimrud – ended the excavation in disappointment, as no large-scale stone monuments were found in Babylon. In 1879, Hormuzd Rassam (1826–1910), a Christian from Mosul who had previously worked with Layard for many years, once again carried out excavations in Babylon on behalf of the British Museum. During the brief period he spent there, he found the famous Kyros Cylinder, which is now in the British Museum, in addition to numerous clay tablets.[15]

French researchers were no less interested in Babylon. They visited the site repeatedly from the 1840s onwards, but initially thought that excavations would be too time-consuming and expensive. Nevertheless, in 1851 they decided to launch a Mesopotamian expedition with the aim of exploring Babylon. This enterprise struggled with major problems from the beginning, and the excavations in Babylon in 1852/53, under the direction of Fulgence Fresnel (1795–1855), did not produce the desired results. Moreover, the ship carrying the archaeological finds sank at *Shatt al-Arab*, the confluence of the Euphrates and Tigris rivers in southern Iraq, on its way back to France. Subsequently the French undertook only small-scale explorations in Babylon. In 1861, the French diplomat Henri-Pacifique Delaporte (1815–1877) visited the ruins and discovered an undisturbed tomb complex from the Parthian period (141 BCE–223 CE); the artefacts from this tomb went to the Louvre.

One undesirable side effect of the growing research interest in Babylon was that large-scale looting took place from the mid-19th century onwards. These artefacts, particularly the clay tablets, found their way via local dealers and middlemen into the European art market. For this reason, today they are scattered all over the world in many different collections.

THE GERMAN EXCAVATIONS, 1899 TO 1917

The excavations in Babylon mark the beginning of German archaeological research in present-day Iraq. While the English and the French had been carrying out large excavations in Mesopotamia since the 1840s and had added numerous artefacts to the collections of their national museums with great fanfare, the Germans only began small-scale explorations after the German Empire was founded in 1871. The beginning of the excavation in Babylon in 1899 was the German Empire's first comparably prestigious archaeological project.

To this day, people often romanticise 19th- and early 20th-century archaeological expeditions, emphasising their pioneering spirit as well as the hardships and dangers they faced. In reality, however, these undertakings were strongly motivated by nationalism, imperialism, and religion. In addition to a sincere interest in bygone cultures, the strategic goal of securing excavation sites and regional supremacy, the acquisition of spectacular finds for their own museums, and – last but not least – the confirmation of biblical stories played an important role in such expeditions. The German interest in Babylon should also be seen in this light. After the German Empire was founded in 1871, national self-confidence and the desire to take on a greater role in foreign policy grew. The young German Empire wanted to expand its political influence in the Ottoman Empire, and at the same time acquire artefacts from Assyria and Babylonia for the museums in Berlin. German scholars of ancient history also feared that without direct access to newly discovered artefacts from Mes-

Fig. 27: Eduard Sachau and Robert Koldewey used a camera to document finding sites during the pre-expedition; this photo shows the Basalt Lion of Babylon, 1897/1898.

opotamia, they would fall behind academically in comparison to Britain and France. As Adolf Erman (1854–1937), the director of the Egyptian Museum at the time, wrote to his friend, the ancient historian and Egyptologist Eduard Meyer (1855–1930), in 1886: "Prussia must dig, so that we are not once again left behind". In 1897 the Academy of Sciences considered the study of Mesopotamia to be one of the most important tasks of the day. Thus from the 1880s onwards, the German Empire made considerable efforts to fill the "gaps" in the collections of the Berlin museums and to catch up with the other major European powers.[16]

Prior to the coronation of Wilhelm II (1859–1941) in 1888, the German Empire had little influence in the region. In the years that followed, Wilhelm II expanded his contacts with the Ottoman Empire and cultivated a friendly relationship with Sultan Abdülhamid II (1842–

1918). The emperor, who was personally very interested in archaeology, used his excellent contacts with the ruler of the Ottoman Empire to obtain excavation licences and to receive allotments of artefacts. He also pursued German economic, political, and military interests in the region. Although Germany was never formally a colonial power in the Near East, the German Empire made use of similar mechanisms and secured political influence as well as excavation permits by means of economic treaties with the Ottoman Empire. Colonialism is not only defined by the formal subordination of certain territories to a colonial power, but is also expressed in an asymmetrical power relationship and the coloniser's idea of their own cultural superiority.[17]

The systematic exploration of Babylon is inseparably linked to the person of Robert Koldewey (see pp. 46–47). This architect and building archaeologist was responsible for se-

Fig. 28: A deciding factor in the choice of Babylon as an excavation site: three unremarkable brick fragments depicting a lion's leg, dragon scales, and cuneiform characters (VA Bab 1498, VA Bab 1499, VA Bab 1500).

lecting Babylon as an excavation site, directing the excavations on site from 1899 to 1917, and subsequently publishing the results. Koldewey had already taken part in the first German expedition to Mesopotamia in 1886/87. The aim of this first expedition was to find a suitable site for a large excavation and to carry out further excavations at two known sites. At that time, such undertakings had no political support in Germany, so the expedition was only possible thanks to the private financing provided by the cotton wholesaler Louis Simon (1828–1903). Due to the level of German influence in the region, which was still quite low at the time, the expedition went anything but smoothly and did not yield the expected results.

It was not until ten years later, in 1897, that a second foray into the exploration of Mesopotamia took place. Alongside the orientalist Eduard Sachau (1845–1930), Koldewey led the so-called pre-expedition, which again set out to look for a suitable site for the first major German excavation project in Mesopotamia (Fig. 27). As no state funds were available, Louis Simon's nephew James Simon (1851–1932), who was also a cotton entrepreneur and one of

the greatest patrons of his time, financed the expedition. While Sachau favoured Ashur – one of the capitals of the Assyrian Empire – for the site of the excavation, Koldewey favoured Babylon. After some back and forth, the committees responsible for the excavation followed Koldewey's recommendation. In addition to the city's well-known name and the associated prestige, the fact that the site had not yet been systematically explored spoke in Babylon's favour. The real deciding factor, however, was the fragments of glazed bricks Koldewey had brought back from Babylon (Fig. 28). As Koldewey wrote to his friend, the archaeologist Otto Puchstein (1856–1911), on 2 August 1898:

Negotiation: Babylon was chosen on the basis of my report, particularly thanks to the brick reliefs I praised.[18]

At that time, Koldewey was already mentioning the possibility of being able to reassemble the brick fragments. In this way he aroused the interest of the museum representatives, since the Louvre was already displaying similar brick reliefs from Susa (Iran). The choice of Babylon was decidedly risky, since earlier missions to the site had not been very successful and the most sensational finds had come mainly from the Assyrian capitals in northern Iraq.

In 1898, the *Deutsche Orient-Gesellschaft* was founded to finance the excavations, and James Simon was the main driving force behind its establishment. Due to the prevailing enthusiasm for the "Orient" at the time, Simon managed to use his excellent network to find a sufficient number of financially sound sponsors for his project within a very short time. In 1901, Emperor Wilhelm II became the patron of the *Deutsche Orient-Gesellschaft* and provided considerable funding for the project. In addition to academic research on the ancient sites, the excavations were also intended to help build up the ancient Near Eastern collections of the Royal Museums in Berlin.

While the project's stated aim was to acquire artefacts for the museums in Berlin, the focus was not on digging for spectacular finds. As an architect, Koldewey particularly emphasised the study of ancient architecture, so the excavations were characterised by a systematic approach and detailed documentation methods (Fig. 29). Koldewey was a pioneer when it came to the difficult work of uncovering the unfired mud bricks typical of Mesopotamia. In addition, he ensured that the contexts of the artefacts were carefully documented, precise maps were drawn up, and technical drawings of the excavation sites were made. The excavation and documentation techniques developed in Babylon were also used in subsequent excavations overseen by the *Deutsche Orient-Gesellschaft* in Mesopotamia. Although the academic yield was great, the artefacts did not meet the expectations of the oversight committees in Germany. In addition, Koldewey's thorough methodology meant that his progress was slower than the donors would have liked.

The team in Babylon carried out excavations all year round, from March 1899 to February 1917. The work was quite strenuous, both for the German staff and for the local excavation workers, particularly during the hot summer months. Even at that time, most other expeditions only worked during the cooler winter months. Koldewey's excavation team consisted of four or five German employees and up to 250 local labourers. The excavations only ended when the British troops approaching Baghdad were just outside Babylon. The artefacts initially remained in the excavation house; the *Deutsche Orient-Gesellschaft* did not reach an agreement on their division with the Kingdom of Iraq until 1926 (see pp. 50–52).

Fig. 29: The Ishtar Gate during the excavation, Babylon 1902.

Robert Koldewey

It is more difficult to get a handle on Robert Koldewey as a person than was the case for some other excavators of his time (Fig. 30). His sober academic writing style revealed hardly any personal details, and he did not leave any memoirs behind. His personal letters – some of which are quite humorous, witty, and biting – provide insights into his personal views, and his student Walter Andrae also published a biography of Koldewey. His contemporaries mostly described him as an introverted, headstrong eccentric.

Johannes Gustav Eduard Robert Koldewey, to give him his full name, was born in Blankenburg in the Harz Mountains in 1855 and grew up in Altona, near Hamburg, from the age of 10. After graduating from secondary school, he studied architecture in Berlin, Vienna, and Munich, and also took courses in archaeology and art history. Beginning in 1877, he worked for some time as a *Regierungsbauführer* (civil architectural engineer) in Hamburg. An unpaid traineeship was a prerequisite for a career as an architect and civil servant in Prussia, which he turned down in favour of an uncertain future as an excavator and a building archaeologist.

In 1882 Koldewey accepted an offer to participate in the exploration of Assos (Turkey) on behalf of the Archaeological Institute of America. Over the next few years, Koldewey undertook several research trips, during which he examined buildings primarily from classical antiquity in present-day Turkey, Greece, and Italy. Since he was only paid for his travel costs – if at all – and not for the evaluation of the artefacts and the publications of his findings, his living situation was extremely precarious for many years.

Fig. 30: Robert Koldewey deciphering a cuneiform inscription on a cylinder, Babylon 1906.

To secure his livelihood, he took a position as a teacher at the *Baugewerkschule* (Building Trades School) in Görlitz from 1895 to 1898 – a job he hated. He first came into contact with ancient Near Eastern cultures in 1886/87, during the first German Mesopotamian expedition. In 1890, 1891, and 1894 he was employed as an architect at the excavation in Zincirli (Turkey), under the direction of Felix von Luschan. The 1897/98 expedition then took him to Mesopotamia for a second time. His appointment as director of the excavation in Babylon seemed to come as a surprise to him, since many people had expected a cuneiform researcher with an outstanding academic reputation to be selected. The fact that the oversight committee chose Koldewey indicated a preference for a practitioner with experience in the region.

In Koldewey's time, most excavators were noblemen, military officers, diplomats, members of trading companies, or priests. Almost none of them had any training in the field of ancient studies, and many lacked any sort of academic interest in their subject. For these men, spectacular finds or proof of biblical narratives were far more important than a scholarly investigation of the sites. By contrast, Koldewey, with his training as an architect, had a much more technical and systematic approach to archaeology than the majority of his contemporaries. He made a particular contribution to the study of mud-brick architecture. Earlier excavators usually failed to recognise the unfired mud bricks and were therefore unable to uncover or document building structures. Thanks to his close observation, Koldewey succeeded in developing a methodology for excavating and documenting this characteristically Mesopotamian construction method.

After he was appointed director of the excavation in Babylon, Koldewey devoted himself completely to researching the site. During the excavation, which lasted about 18 years, he returned to Germany only three times, and for short periods (in 1904, 1910, and 1914). When the war forced him to end the excavation in 1917, he kept himself busy until his death in 1925 publishing the results of those years of field research in Babylon. In addition to extensive academic publications, *Das wieder erstehende Babylon* (lit. "Babylon Reborn", published in English translation as *The Excavations at Babylon*) was also published while the excavation was ongoing. The book was a great success and made the results of the excavation accessible to a broad audience.

Due to the method he developed for recording the buildings – that is, the documentation of architectural remains – Koldewey is still considered one of the founders of modern building archaeology. A year after his death, his students and colleagues founded the *Arbeitsgemeinschaft archäologischer Architekten* (Archaeological Architects Working Group), which they named the *Koldewey-Gesellschaft* (Koldewey Society) in his honour.

BABYLON FROM 1917 UNTIL TODAY – EXCAVATIONS AND RESTORATIONS

The large-scale Western excavations – in which foreign excavators were granted a large share of the artefacts, which were divided up – came to a definitive end with the Second World War. From then on, with a few exceptions, most excavations were smaller and the majority of the artefacts remained in the country. The *Deutsche Archäologische Institut* (German Archaeological Institute) excavated in Babylon from 1956 to 1972, but on a much smaller scale than the earlier German excavations. An Italian team worked in the southern area of the city from 1987 to 1989. The Iraq State Board of Antiquities and Heritage carried out more extensive excavations from 1978, in connection with a major restoration project.

Fig. 31: An English company filming about tourism in Arab countries, as captured by the Iraqi photographer Latif al Ani (1961).

After the war forced Koldewey to end his excavations in 1917, the excavation team left the exposed remains of the buildings unprotected, and the excavation trenches as well as the mud-brick architecture increasingly deteriorated. In subsequent years, Babylon became a frequently visited site, attracting both domestic and foreign tourists (Fig. 31). For this reason, by the 1940s the Iraq State Board of Antiquities and Heritage had already begun to reconstruct individual buildings onsite and to erect a replica of the Ishtar Gate in the city centre (Fig. 32). Despite these measures, the huge site remained confusing and unattractive, and a visit to Babylon was probably a disappointment to most tourists.

An extensive restoration programme in Babylon began under Saddam Hussein in 1978 and changed Babylon's entire cityscape. The work included academic excavations and primarily focussed on conservation measures. In addition, the Iraq State Board of Antiquities and Heritage used new bricks to rebuild Nebuchadnezzar II's huge Southern Palace atop the remains of the original building (see pp. 64–66). This undertaking was controversial, however, since the modern reconstruction constituted a major encroachment on the site.

Babylon experienced a sad low point in its recent history during the Second Iraq War in 2003, when American and Polish troops established a base in the centre of the ancient city. Over approximately one year of military use, the site suffered severe damage: the troops dug trenches through archaeological layers and damaged structures – the Ishtar Gate and the Processional Way in particular. Following massive international protests, the base closed in 2004, and Iraq regained control of Babylon. Since 2007, the Iraq State Board of Antiquities and Heritage and the World Monuments Fund have carried out restoration projects, which aim to repair recent damage and to restore the site to its authentic state. With its designation as a World Heritage Site on 5 July 2019, UNESCO granted Babylon a special status that is intended to protect the ruins over the long term (see p. 66).

Even though no extensive archaeological excavations have taken place in Babylon in recent years, research into the city and its culture continues. Museums in Baghdad, Istanbul, London, and Berlin hold numerous archaeological artefacts and cuneiform texts that have not yet been comprehensively analysed. Due to the long history of excavations since the mid-19th century, the sheer number of artefacts, and the extensive restoration work onsite, research on

Fig. 32: The replica of the Ishtar Gate in Babylon.

Babylon is extremely complex and can only be managed today within the framework of international academic cooperation.

---

9 Herodotus (1920), *The Persian Wars, Vol. 1: Books 1–2*, transl. A. D. Godley (Loeb Classical Library 117; Cambridge, MA: Harvard University Press).

10 The corresponding passage is found in Diodorus Siculus, *Bibliotheca historica*, II 8, quoting 4. An overview of Cteslas's description of Babylon and its historical classification is provided in Jacobs 2011; see also Rollinger in Marzahn and Schauerte 2008: 499–500.

11 For further details on Berossos's accounts of construction activities in Babylon, see Rollinger in Marzahn and Schauerte 2008: 501–502; Rollinger 2013.

12 Accounts of the Hanging Gardens can be found in Diodorus Siculus, II 7–9; Strabo, *Geographica* XVI, 1, 5–6; and particularly Quintus Curtius Rufus, V 1.17–39.

13 Corresponding accounts can be found in Strabo, *Geographica* XVI, 1, 5–6; and Pliny the Elder, *Naturalis Historia* VI, 26.

14 This passage, taken from a report by de Beauchamp, is reproduced in Rich 1839: 302, no. 6.

15 An excellent overview of the discovery and historical classification as well as the translation of the so-called Kyros Cylinder can be found in Finkel 2013.

16 The comprehensive exhibition catalogue "Das Grosse Spiel" (Trümpler 2008) was devoted to the topic of archaeology and politics. On Emperor Wilhelm II and his interest in archaeology, see Beigel and Mangold 2017, with further references.

17 The definition of colonialism, and especially its distinction from imperialism, is a controversial scholarly issue. The classification used here is oriented towards the text "Guidelines for the Care of Collections from Colonial Contexts" (2021) by the *Deutschen Museumsbundes* (German Museums Association).

FROM BABYLON TO BERLIN

HOW THE BABYLONIAN BRICKS CAME TO BERLIN – DIVIDING AND TRANS-PORTING THE ARTEFACTS

In 1884 the Ottoman Empire enacted a new Antiquities Law, according to which all the empire's antiquities became state property. This largely prevented the division of archaeological artefacts between the Ottoman Empire and foreign excavators, which had been stipulated by law until that time. In order to secure some artefacts for the museums in Berlin despite this new law, the excavators had been working alongside representatives at the highest political level in Germany since the beginning of the excavations to secure a special arrangement. The glazed brick fragments played a central role in these negotiations.

Just a few months after the excavation began in June 1899, Koldewey aimed to export the brick fragments that had already been collected so they could be more extensively studied in Berlin. At that time, reconstructing the depictions on the glazed brick reliefs was not yet a possibility. Thus in November 1899, he still presumed that the brick fragments had probably once formed the panelling on a corridor wall and depicted hunting scenes. Perhaps individual brick fragments had reminded him of the Neo-Assyrian reliefs, which were well known at the time, and which often depicted hunting scenes. In the subsequent period, Koldewey's assistant, Walter Andrae (see pp. 62–63), suc-

ceeded in drawing reconstructions first of one of the lions on the Processional Way, and eventually of the bulls and the dragons on the Ishtar Gate as well.

Osman Hamdi Bey (see pp. 53–54), the head of the Ottoman Antiquities Administration, finally agreed to export the bricks to Berlin. On 2 September 1902, he wrote to Richard Schöne (1840–1920), the general director of the Royal Museums in Berlin:

Today I find myself in a position to inform you that the management of the Imperial Museum has agreed with Your Excellency that all the numerous fragments of glazed bricks discovered during the Babylon excavations may be transported to Berlin to be scientifically and artistically assembled and restored, and subsequently returned to the Imperial Museum.[19]

Hamdi Bey, who was familiar with Andrae's colourful watercolours, saw the great added value of the reassembled brick reliefs and emphasised the academic and artistic aspect of the reconstruction in his letter. One of the conditions for the export was that half of the reassembled relief animals be returned to the Ottoman Empire once they were complete. In March 1903, the Sublime Porte, the seat of the Ottoman government, officially agreed to the export, and on 12 May 1903, 399 crates of brick fragments began their long journey from Babylon to Berlin (Fig. 33). As agreed, the German authorities re-

Fig. 33: Original transport crates with glazed brick fragments. The glazed bricks arrived in Berlin in this condition in 1927.

turned half of the completed animals to Istanbul in subsequent years. By 1930, 13 relief animals had reached the Istanbul Archaeological Museum, where they are still on display today.

When the excavation came to its unplanned end in February 1917, hundreds more crates of bricks, as well as thousands of other artefacts, remained in the excavation house in Babylon (see p. 45). The Ottoman Empire – which once stretched from the Caspian Sea to Hungary in the north, Algeria in the west, and Yemen in the south – had already forfeited its dominance in the region and lost large parts of its territory in the 19th century. After its defeat in the First World War, the empire finally disintegrated, and large areas remained under Allied control. France and Britain had already concluded the secret Sykes–Picot Agreement in 1916, in which they divided the Arab provinces of the Ottoman

Empire between themselves. Syria and Lebanon fell to France, while Palestine and present-day Jordan and Iraq went to Great Britain. After several uprisings and rebellions, the British installed Faisal I as king in Iraq in 1921. The Kingdom of Iraq remained a British Mandate until 1932 and was thus politically, economically, and strategically dependent on Britain.[20]

The newly founded Iraqi Antiquities Service, under its British director Gertrude Bell (see pp. 54–55), began negotiations with Berlin in 1926 – nine years after the excavations ended – about the finds stored in Babylon. Once again, the brick fragments played a central role in this agreement. Negotiating an agreement on these artefacts was also in the interests of the Iraqi Antiquities Service at the time, because artefacts from Babylon would also be displayed in the newly established National Museum in

Figs. 34–36: Packing the finds at the excavation house, transporting the crates by sailboat to Hilla, and then transferring them to the train, 1926.

Baghdad. Bell instigated the division of artefacts according to the new Iraqi Antiquities Law, which once again provided for a division of the artefacts between the Kingdom of Iraq and the foreign excavators.[21]

The *Deutsche Orient-Gesellschaft* commissioned Andrae, Koldewey's former assistant in Babylon and curator of the *Vorderasiatische Abteilung*, to carry out the division of artefacts on its behalf. Andrae travelled to Iraq in the autumn of 1926. After Bell's unexpected death in July 1926, Abd el Kadr Patschatschi, the curator of the Iraq Museum, supervised the division of the artefacts in Babylon. Transporting the

crates of artefacts proved to be an adventure: the workmen first brought them from Babylon to nearby Hilla in small sailboats, where they then transferred them to freight cars (Figs. 34–36). The finds destined for the Iraq Museum travelled north to Baghdad, and the Berlin boxes went to Basra in southern Iraq. From there they sailed by steamer to Hamburg, and in 1927 some 400 crates of glazed brick fragments finally reached Berlin, along with other artefacts. After the conservators restored them, the museum in Berlin sent one example each of a lion, a dragon, and a bull reconstructed from original fragments back to the Iraq Museum in Baghdad.

Osman Hamdi Bey and Gertrude Bell

Osman Hamdi Bey (1842–1910) and Gertrude Bell (1868–1926) played leading roles in negotiating the agreement on who would receive the glazed brick fragments from Babylon. As different as their backgrounds and motivations were, they were both among the most interesting and influential cultural and political actors in the Near East at the turn of the century.

Hamdi Bey was a painter, excavator, museum director, and (cultural) politician (Fig. 37). He was born into an influential family in Istanbul in 1842. In 1860 his father sent him to France to study law. During his nine-year stay in Paris, however, Hamdi Bey devoted himself primarily to art, and particularly to painting. His teachers included Gustave Boulanger (1824–1888) and Jean-Léon Gérôme (1824–1904), two of the most important representatives of French Orientalism. Hamdi Bey primarily painted scenes of everyday Ottoman life, which differed from contemporary European depictions of the Orient (Fig. 39). His works are included in the collections of numerous important museums. Two of his large-scale paintings hang in the entrance

Fig. 37: Osman Hamdi Bey.

Fig. 38: Gertrude Bell in front of her tent, probably in Babylon, April 1909 (K_218).

hall of the *Alte Nationalgalerie* (Old National Gallery) in Berlin.

Back in Istanbul, Hamdi Bey worked in the diplomatic service and served in the Ottoman province of Baghdad from 1869 to 1871. During this time he developed an interest in archaeology and subsequently undertook excavations at Sidon (Lebanon) and Nemrut Dağı (Turkey). After accepting a series of positions in the administration, he was finally appointed director of the Müze-i Humayun (Imperial Museum), now the Istanbul Archaeological Museum, in 1891. He remained in this position until his death in 1910, making him *de facto* the most powerful man in the Ottoman Empire in the fields of archaeology, art, and culture. Hamdi Bey is largely responsible for the new Ottoman Antiquities Law of 1884, which de-

clared all antiquities to be state property and thus put a stop to the unregulated export of ancient cultural objects. This law would subsequently become the model for numerous other antiquities laws in the region.

Gertrude Bell was an explorer, a writer, an archaeologist, a British Secret Service employee, a museum director, a politician, and much more (Fig. 38). Her unusual life provided material for numerous documentaries and romanticised feature films. Gertrude Margaret Lowthian Bell was born on 14 July 1868, the eldest daughter of Sir Hugh Bell, a very wealthy and progressive English aristocrat. This enabled her to begin her studies at Oxford in 1886, whence she graduated with the highest honours in 1888. She was not awarded an academic title, however, as this privilege was reserved exclusively for men at Oxford until 1920. Over the next several years she travelled extensively, and between 1899 and 1914 she spent long periods in the Near East, where she increasingly turned her attention to archaeology. She wrote about her experiences and her research in various books. In 1908 she travelled to present-day Iraq and visited the German excavations at Ashur, among other places. She was very impressed by the meticulous methods of the excavators working there and remained on friendly terms with the director of the excavation, Walter Andrae, for the rest of her life (see pp. 62–63).

During the First World War, Bell worked for the British intelligence services, first in Cairo (Egypt) and then in Basra (Iraq). The Ottoman Empire was allied with the German Empire and thus an enemy of Great Britain during the war. With her excellent knowledge of languages and locales, as well as numerous personal contacts

with various Arab tribes, she was a useful resource for the British military. When the Allies won the war, 400 years of Ottoman suzerainty in Mesopotamia came to an end. Bell was instrumental in the reorganisation of the region and subsequently in the establishment of the Kingdom of Iraq in 1921, which was under the British Mandate until 1932. During this period, Bell was responsible for archaeology. From 1922 she was in charge of the Iraqi Antiquities Service. She was the director of the newly established Iraq National Museum in Baghdad from 1925 until her death, and she also initiated the first Iraqi Antiquities Law, which came into force in 1924. In contrast to the older Ottoman Antiquities Law, this law once again provided for the division of artefacts and thus accommodated foreign archaeologists. On 12 July 1926, Bell died of an overdose of sleeping pills in Baghdad, where she is buried.

Fig. 39: "Turkish Street Scene" by Osman Hamdi Bey (1888) (ANG A I420).

FROM FRAGMENT TO MONUMENT – RECONSTRUCTING THE ISHTAR GATE

When the Pergamon Museum first opened its doors to the public in 1930, the grand Babylonian architectural reconstructions – the Ishtar Gate, the Processional Way, and the Throne Room Façade – were among the highlights, and they remain so to this day. Realising these spectacular reconstructions required a great deal of knowledge, effort, and persuasion. The success of this project was due first and foremost to the untiring commitment and artistic skill of Walter Andrae (see pp. 62–63). Even while he was still onsite at the excavation in Babylon, he had already reconstructed individual animals representing the gods in drawings he made based on small fragments. As director of the *Vorderasiatische Abteilung*, he was largely responsible for the reconstruction of the gate in the Pergamon Museum.

Before any thought could be given to assembling the relief animals, the brick fragments first had to be elaborately prepared. When the first fragments arrived in Berlin in 1903, the first director of the Chemical Laboratory of the Royal Museums in Berlin, Friedrich Rathgen, immediately examined them. The chemical analyses revealed that damaging salts had accumulated in the bricks during the approximately 2,500 years they were buried in the soil. Once the excavators freed the fragments from the soil, these salts began to bloom and thus destroyed the glazes. Therefore the bricks had to be thoroughly desalinated before they were put together. To accomplish this, the laboratory staff placed the fragments in 230 large wine barrels filled with water and changed the water regularly over sev-

eral weeks (Fig. 40). Afterwards they reinforced the glazes with wax. In this way, they desalinated all the brick fragments within 18 months. Workers subsequently sorted the brick fragments according to colour and motif, and reassembled them on the basis of the drawings Andrae had made during the excavation (Figs. 41–42). Thus in 1906, the team completed the first two lions, one of which was immediately sent to Istanbul. Over the following years, the team created further individual relief animals.

Andrae, who was still working in Ashur at the time, visited Berlin in 1908 and was appalled by the way in which the reconstruction had been carried out. Instead of assembling matching fragments, the workers had sawn the fragments so that the edges fit neatly together. They covered the missing sections with oil paint to make the reliefs look "new". When Andrae finally took over as director of the *Vorderasiatische Abteilung* in 1928, he had the relief animals reconstructed according to his own ideas. In this process, the conservation team left the fragments in their original form and shaped the missing parts to fit the original relief. They did not adapt the modern additions to match the colouring of the original glazes, leaving them clay-coloured instead. Thus – if one looks closely – the original fragments and the modern additions can still be clearly distinguished today.

The elaborate reconstruction in the Pergamon Museum required Andrae to do a lot of convincing. Due to the extensive amount of work and the high cost involved, he was initially refused permission to reconstruct the entire gate and could only recreate a pair of each of the animals. Nevertheless, Andrae and the responsible managing architect, Wilhelm Wille, kindled the donors' imaginations in an unusual way: they hired scene painters from the State Opera House and created the Ishtar Gate out of wood and paper in the skeleton of the Pergamon Museum.

With a few watercolours I had tried to jog the museum architects' limited imagination by providing perspective and colour (Fig. 43). The ministry, which had granted the money, also had to be prompted, and in the most readily understandable way possible: in the original size! The managing architect Wille was so impressed by my perspective of the Ishtar Gate that he had it built out of wood in its original size and then covered with paper, on which the scene painters from the State Opera House had to paint my bulls and dragons, true to life and with shadowing – it was a pleasure to look upon it (Fig. 44). The ministers, who had previously only wanted to approve a single pair of each animal because they were all "the same", were so moved by this theatre mock-up that they immediately approved everything (W. Andrae, *Lebenserinnerungen eines Ausgräbers*, p. 276).

Fig. 40: First, the bricks had to be thoroughly desalinated. To accomplish this, the staff at the Chemical Laboratory of the Royal Museums placed the fragments in barrels of water, which they changed regularly (1928).

Fig. 41: Staff sorting and assembling the brick fragments. Walter Andrae's hand-drawn reconstructions of the animals in their original size hang on the wall to the right (1928/1929).

Fig. 42: Using a mould to assemble a brick from the inscription. The missing sections were filled in with plaster, and the cuneiform characters were later completed with paint (1929/1930).

Fig. 43: Design for the reconstruction of the Ishtar Gate in the Pergamon Museum. Watercolour by Walter Andrae, 1927.

From then on, they worked relentlessly on the brick reliefs. Within just two years, the sculptor Willy Struck and a team of up to 30 workers assembled 72 relief animals. Since the available original brick fragments were not sufficient for the planned reconstruction in the museum, Andrae looked for a way to fill in the empty spaces. To this end, in 1928 he commissioned the ceramic manufacturers Richard Mutz, Richard Blumenfeld, and Helene Körting to produce glazed bricks (Fig. 45). While both Mutz and Blumenfeld are well known in the specialist literature and works from the Mutz ceramic factory were even shown in a solo exhibition in 2002, we know very little about Körting's workshops in Oranienburg. Yet Andrae felt that the glazes from her workshops, which were used on the Processional Way and the Throne Room Façade, were particularly successful.

In the 1920s and 1930s, Körting was one of the most outstanding ceramicists in Germany. In addition to producing ceramics for gardens and buildings, she also accepted artistic commissions. For example, together with Mies van der Rohe and Wassily Kandinsky, she designed a music room at the Berlin Architecture Exhibition in 1931, turning one of Kandinsky's designs into ceramic wall panelling. Producing bricks for the Ishtar Gate was an extremely prestigious and lucrative commission for her up-and-coming workshops.

One can imagine how passionately we potters welcomed the project. We were allowed to carry the real chunks into our laboratories as research material, to trace the magic of the mysterious turquoise and the luminosity of the cobalt blue with our eyes and fingers, down to their finest details (H. Körting, *Keramische Zeitschrift* [1955], p. 623).

The particular challenge was that the modern bricks could not outshine the antique ones – that is, they had to look "old". In addition, the glaze on the Babylonian bricks is extremely thick, and one would preferably want to avoid this when creating modern glazes. In order to achieve the desired effect and play of colour, Körting experimented with various additives. Her correspondence with Andrae, together with two extensive articles published in ceramics journals, prove how deeply she was concerned with the Babylonian glazes. As she wrote in one of her journal articles:

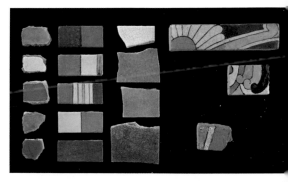

Fig. 45: Glaze samples produced by Körting, Blumenfeld, and Mutz for the reconstruction of the Ishtar Gate, the Processional Way, and the so-called Throne Room Façade, with an original fragment as a reference (1928/1929).

The main difficulty was that the luminosity of the old bricks is severely dimmed by the numerous fracture seams. Therefore the luminosity of individual fragments could not be used as an archetype, but rather the effect of the reassembled brick, without imitating the fracture seams in the new bricks (H. Körting, *Keramische Rundschau* [1930], p. 652).

Blumenfeld and Mutz probably also benefited from Körting's knowledge of Babylonian glazes, so it is largely thanks to her that the reconstructions of the Ishtar Gate, the Processional Way, and the Throne Room Façade present such a harmonious and unified effect today. Both the blue background and the ornamental bands, the floral patterns and the battlements on the Ishtar Gate, the Throne Room Façade, and the

Fig. 44: The first replica of the Ishtar Gate, made of wood and paper, in the Pergamon Museum (1928/1929).

Fig. 46: Erecting the substructure of the Ishtar Gate in the museum (1929/1930).

mine only the ground plan, since the walls of the earliest construction phase are still standing. For the reconstruction, Andrae drew on ancient depictions – which most likely do not actually depict the gates of Babylon – as well as general proportional considerations and findings from the two earlier construction phases. On the other hand, the height of the gate and the towers; the design of the gate's passages, battlements, and windows; and the arrangement of the individual animals and the ornamental bands are all largely unknown. Only the front gate, not the entire double gate structure, is reproduced in the Pergamon Museum (Fig. 46). The entire 50 x 22–28 metre gate structure would not have fit in the museum. Instead, the team only built one section, which was based on the smaller front part of the gate. This measures 4.38 x 26.41 metres, in line with the ground plan, and is 14.75 metres high.[22] The visionary reconstruction of the Ishtar Gate in Berlin is therefore less a representation of Nebuchadnezzar II's original gate than a modern impression of how we can imagine the entire gate structure looked in Babylon in the 6th century BCE. Thus the reconstruction primarily reflects the ideas of the excavators and the team at the museum.

The Pergamon Museum opened on 2 October 1930, giving the public the opportunity to marvel at the reconstructed large-scale Babylonian architecture. In addition to the Pergamon Altar and the Market Gate of Miletus, the Ishtar Gate and the Processional Way were the main attractions at the museum. Visitors were particularly fascinated by the vivid colour of the Babylonian glazed bricks. However, critical voices also had their say. They called into question not only the immense costs of the project under dif-

Processional Way consist almost entirely of these same modern bricks. Less than 20 per cent of the Ishtar Gate, about 45 per cent of the Processional Way, and as little as 15 per cent of the Throne Room Façade are composed of original Babylonian bricks. It was solely in the cases of the animals – the lions, dragons, and bulls – that the conservators only had to add small sections.

While the shape of the gods' representative animals in relief is known from the older models, we know very little about the original appearance of the entire gate. We can precisely deter-

ficult economic conditions, but also the idea of displaying exterior architecture in interior spaces. In 1939, after only a few years, the Second World War forced the exhibition to close. While the staff stored all the movable exhibits safely in the museum's basement, they could not simply remove and relocate the architectural reconstructions. They remained in the exhibition hall, and museum staff walled them in or protected them with sandbags.

In November 1943, the Allies flew extensive air raids over Berlin. On 26 November 1943, a bomb hit the Pergamon Museum and destroyed the roof in the area over the Processional Way and the Ishtar Gate. One of the gate's towers was severely damaged (Fig. 47). Fortunately this section was made entirely of modern bricks and could be restored after the war. But it was not possible to repair the roof – not even in a makeshift fashion – until the end of 1946. In 1951 the glass roof was replaced and the architecture exhibition halls were once again opened to the public. Two years later, the other rooms in the *Vorderasiatisches Museum* were also opened to the public. Due to the damage the roof had sustained, the glazed bricks had been exposed to the weather for at least three years, and the invasive moisture proved to be particularly damaging for the glazes. For this reason, the

Fig. 47: War damage along the Processional Way in the *Vorderasiatisches Museum* (1946).

museum's conservators check the architectural reconstructions several times a year – even now, 80 years after the bomb hit – and immediately reinforce loose glaze fragments.

18 A complete transcript of the letter, dated 2 August 1898, is reproduced in Quatember and Bankel 2018: 189–190.
19 A transcript of the entire letter in the original French can be found in Crüsemann 2000: 284, doc. 8.
20 On the formation and development of the British Mandate in Iraq, see Tripp 2007: 30–74.
21 A good chronological overview of cultural protection laws in Iraq can be found at https://saving-antiquities.org/laenderinformation/irak (accessed 4 February 2022). For more detailed information on the Iraqi Antiquities Law of 1924, see Bernhardsson 2005: 112–129.
22 The front gate of the oldest construction phase that has been preserved was 13 x 28 metres, about 1.5 metres longer and 8.6 metres deeper than the reconstruction in the Pergamon Museum. For further information on the dimensions of the gateway, see Pedersén 2020: 71–72.

Walter Andrae

The reconstruction of the Ishtar Gate is primarily Walter Andrae's (1875–1956) achievement. Andrae spent more than 30 years of his life grappling with the architectural reconstructions that appear in the Pergamon Museum today (Fig. 48). The young architect gained his first experience as Koldewey's assistant in Babylon. From the very beginning of the excavation, Koldewey entrusted the newcomer with the documentation of the glazed bricks because Andrae's drawing skills had caught his eye. In less than a year, Andrae succeeded in reconstructing the lions along the Processional Way from small pieces of glazed brick (Fig. 49).

Andrae was born to a middle-class family in Anger, near Leipzig, on 18 February 1875. His talent for drawing was apparent at an early age, but he was only encouraged in this during his architectural studies at the Technical University of Dresden from 1893 to 1898. Thanks to his sister, the painter Elisabeth Andrae (1876–1945), he also had access to artistic circles. After his studies he passed the state examination and qualified as a *Regierungsbauführer* (civil architectural engineer), which would have opened up a career as a civil servant in Prussia. After working for the *Staatsbauamt* (State Construction Office) for a few weeks, he answered an advertisement for a job as a draughtsman on an expedition to the Near East. In 1899, at the age of 24, with almost no professional experience and no knowledge of the region or the language, he set out with Koldewey on a journey to Babylon. At Emperor Wilhelm II's request, they recorded the ruins of Baalbek in present-day Lebanon on the way. As

Fig. 48: Walter Andrae, 1935.

Koldewey wrote to his friend Otto Puchstein at the time:

He (namely the assistant) makes the sketch, but I have to give him almost every line, every measure that is necessary, as a novice he cannot distinguish the important from the unimportant. [...] He does an excellent job at watercolours and drawing! (after Quatember and Bankel [2018], pp. 202–203).

But Andrae learned quickly, and as early as 1901 Koldewey put him in charge of the excavations in Borsippa, Fara, and for a time in Babylon. From 1903 to 1914 he directed the excavation in Ashur, the second major *Deutsche Orient-Gesellschaft* excavation project in present-day Iraq. Andrae maintained a close relationship with his teacher and mentor Koldewey throughout his life.

Immediately after his return from Ashur in 1914, Andrae was drafted into military service and initially deployed as a company commander in the trenches in France. Due to his local knowledge and language skills, he was dispatched to the Mesopotamian front in 1915. Between 1915 and 1918, he was stationed as an officer in Turkey, Syria, Iran, Palestine, and above all in what is now Iraq. However, little is known about his precise activities during the war in Mesopotamia. According to Andrae's autobiography, written in 1955 and published after his death, he was mainly responsible for logistical tasks.

In 1921 Andrae succeeded Koldewey as the officer in charge of external affairs at the Berlin Museums' *Vorderasiatische Abteilung* and devoted the subsequent years primarily to the publication of his findings from the excavation in Ashur. In the autumn of 1926 he returned to Iraq to oversee the division of the finds from the Babylon excavation (see pp. 50–52). Shortly prior to this, he had also succeeded in bringing the artefacts from Ashur – which had been stuck in Portugal throughout the First World War – to Berlin. After then-director Otto Weber's sudden death in 1928, Andrae became the new director of the *Vorderasiatische Abteilung* and was thus largely responsible for designing the exhibition in the Pergamon Museum. His particular contribution was the realisation of the architectural reconstructions, which still contribute to the unique character of the *Vorderasiatisches Museum* today (see pp. 66–67).

Fig. 49: The first reconstruction of a lion from the Processional Way. The artefact numbers of the individual brick fragments are noted in red. Drawing by Walter Andrae, 1899.

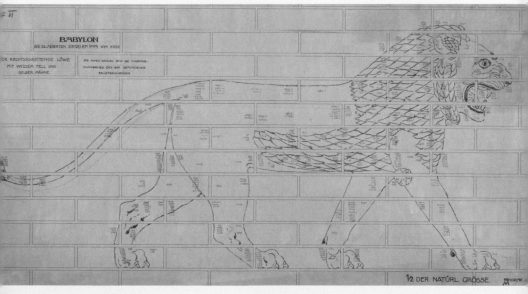

THE SIGNIFICANCE AND PRESERVATION OF A PIECE OF WORLD CULTURAL HERITAGE

THE ISHTAR GATE IN IRAQ

Babylon – and the Ishtar Gate in particular – have great symbolic meaning for Iraq. When the kingdom was founded in 1921, an ethnically and religiously heterogeneous state emerged. For the various groups that made up the population, pre-Islamic cultural heritage was a common point of identification. Over the years, the importance of the ancient Mesopotamian cultures for the young state's national identity steadily increased.[23]

From the late 1970s onwards, Saddam Hussein (1937–2006) increasingly referred to Iraq's pre-Islamic heritage by identifying himself with the Assyrian and Babylonian kings and setting himself up as the direct successor of these "ancient Oriental" rulers.[24] He also promoted

Fig. 50: The ruins of Babylon in March 2017. On the right is Nebuchadnezzar II's reconstructed royal palace (Southern Palace), on the left Saddam Hussein's palace on an artificial hill, and in the background the Euphrates.

Fig. 51: A brick displaying Saddam Hussein's building inscription.

archaeological undertakings and completed extensive restoration projects. Babylon and its monumental buildings constituted a particular focal point. In 1978, the Iraq State Board of Antiquities and Heritage began a large-scale restoration and excavation project in Babylon (see pp. 47–49).

In addition to excavations and restorative measures, the project included the creation of lakes and gardens as well as three huge artificial mounds. Saddam Hussein had a monumental palace built on one of these hills (Fig. 50). Furthermore, he also rebuilt various ancient buildings – such as Nebuchadnezzar II's Southern Palace, parts of the city wall, and certain sanctuaries – with modern bricks. Taking inspiration from the building inscriptions on Nebuchadnezzar II's bricks, Saddam Hussein produced bricks with his own inscription on them. In contrast to its ancient forebears, this inscription is written in Arabic, and the bricks arc built into the masonry in a way that allows the inscription to be seen (Fig. 51). It reads:

Under the rule of the victorious Saddam Hussein, the president of the Republic – may God preserve him – the protector of great Iraq, the innovator of its revival, and the builder of its great culture; the restoration of the great city of Babylon was completed in 1987.

For Saddam Hussein, the project was less about historical authenticity than about demonstrating Babylon's grandeur and splendour to visitors. He also used the ancient ruins for events. Concerts and receptions were held in Nebuchadnezzar II's throne room, while up to 2,500 people could be seated in the specially restored Greek theatre. From 1987 onwards, a grandiose international Babylon Festival was held almost every year. The site of the ruins was also a popular destination for excursions, and the general population was very much aware of them. In addition, various banknotes depicted the Ishtar Gate and other ancient motifs.

To this day, Babylon and the Ishtar Gate in particular arc profoundly important to the Iraqi population, which is why its use as a military base by American and Polish troops during the 2003 Iraq War was seen as a provocation and was also deeply hurtful. Comprehensive documentation taken immediately after the troops withdrew revealed massive damage to the archaeological structures. Work to repair the damage is still underway: in 2010, under the direction of the Iraq State Board of Antiquities and Heritage and in cooperation with the World Monuments Fund, restoration work began on the remaining parts of the Ishtar Gate. The aim of these measures is not only to repair recent damage caused by military use, but also to permanently secure the architectural remains. A careful investigation revealed that the high groundwater level in particular poses a danger to the structure. As a result of earlier restoration measures, water was dammed up in the area around the Ishtar Gate. To protect the gate, these interventions had to be partly revised. Thanks to these measures, the water now drains away better. Another of the project's goals is to develop Babylon for tourism in an appropriate manner, which simultaneously guarantees the protection of the ruins. However, sustainable site management for such a large urban area as Babylon involves immense logistical and financial challenges.

Thus it is all the more gratifying that UNESCO added Babylon to its list of World Heritage Sites on 5 July 2019. This status recognises the ancient city's historical significance and places the site under protection. UNESCO's justification is as follows:

Babylon is an archaeological site which stands out as a unique testimony to one of the most influential empires of the ancient world [...] Babylon radiated not only political, technical and artistic influence over all regions of the ancient Near and Middle East, but it also left a considerable scientific legacy in the fields of mathematics and astronomy.

THE ISHTAR GATE IN BERLIN

The history of the Ishtar Gate and the Processional Way in Berlin did not end when the Pergamon Museum opened in 1930 or when museum staff repaired the damage after the Second World War (see pp. 60–61). In 1999 UNESCO designated Museum Island and its five buildings as a World Heritage Site. This means that the reconstruction of the Ishtar Gate, the Processional Way, and the Throne Room Façade have also taken on special significance.

It is not only the freestanding walls of the Ishtar Gate in Babylon that require regular restoration; the reconstructions in Berlin also necessitate permanent conservation and care in order to preserve these outstanding monuments over the long term. To this end, conservators thoroughly inspect all the glazed brick façades several times a year in order to detect changes

Fig. 52: Sonja Radujkovic, a conservator at the *Vorderasiatisches Museum*, performing the routine check of the Processional Way with a microscope.

and potential damage at an early stage (Fig. 52). They also clean the glazed brick façades twice a year and remove the dust with fine brushes. Every ten years or so the façades require a comprehensive conservation process, which lasts several months and during which loose glaze fragments at risk of detaching from the structure are stabilised. During the most recent restoration of the Processional Way in 2020, conservators removed the post-war restorations. Due to the difficult conditions just after the war, previous conservators could not pay as much attention to artistic detail; neither the shape nor the colour of these post-war restorations blended coherently into the overall impression. The new, carefully executed additions are again more closely oriented to the original work done in 1930 (Fig. 53).

As part of the general renovation of the Pergamon Museum, the Ishtar Gate, the Processional Way, and the Throne Room Façade will also be comprehensively restored, but will be preserved in their original condition. Since it is not possible to remove these sensitive large-scale architectural monuments without causing damage, they will remain in the building during the construction work and will be protected by sophisticated technology. A measuring system

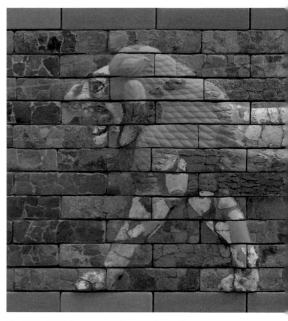

Fig. 53: In this lion's mane, which was newly supplemented in 2020, the original and the modern sections are clearly separated.

will sound the alarm if shocks or vibrations occur, even before they reach a level that would be dangerous for the objects. In addition, the architectural reconstructions will receive a climate-controlled, dust-free protective casing.

---

23 I can only briefly touch on the complex issue of the colonial founding of the state of Iraq in 1921, the struggle for sovereignty, and the resulting identity formation here. For further information, see, for example, Baram 1991; Bernhardsson 2005: 164–221; Seymour 2016: 235–248.

24 On the other hand, Bahrani (1998) points out that the image of the Oriental despot continues to have an impact in the West today, and Middle Eastern heads of state are frequently portrayed as dictators and despots with reference to ancient Near Eastern kings.

IMPACT AND RECEPTION

BABYLON – BETWEEN HISTORY AND LEGEND

The name Babylon evokes a variety of associations: the Tower of Babylon/Babel, the Babylonian Exile, the Hanging Gardens, the whore of Babylon, the city of witchcraft and wine, the Babylonian confusion of languages, and much more. The city served as a projection screen for various cultures and religions, and Babylon's image changed according to the time and the context. In the process, myths and ideas about Babylon have superseded the former ancient city.

The very name Babylon blends history and myth. Since little is known about the city's humble beginnings, a rich collection of legends arose early on (see p. 8). Sparse evidence points to an original city name of *Ba(b)bar* or *Ba(b)bal*. Due to the similar sound, this later became *Bābili*, which in Akkadian meant "gate of the god" and underlined Babylon's claim to be a religious centre. The Hebrew Bible (*Tanakh*)[25] plays with the city's name, transcribing it not as *Bāb'el* (בבאל), which would be "gate of God" in Aramaic, but as *Bābel* (בבל), which means confusion or commingling. This is an allusion to the Babylonian confusion of languages. As the Bible puts it:

Therefore it was called Babel, because there the Lord confused the language of all the earth; and from there the Lord scattered them abroad over the face of all the earth (Genesis 11:9).

Arabic adopted something close to this form, which is why the place is still called *Bābil* (بابل) today. In the 19th and early 20th centuries, the biblical Hebrew name Babel was still common, while today we mostly use the spelling Babylon, which traces back to its Greek name.

Babylon plays a role in the scriptures of Judaism, Christianity, and Islam. Our Eurocentric concept of Babylon is therefore strongly influenced by the biblical tradition, which paints a consistently negative picture of the city. Babylon is portrayed in the Bible as the corrupt capital of a morally degenerate empire (Fig. 54). Almost all the direct references to Babylon in the Bible refer to the Neo-Babylonian and Persian periods in the 6th century BCE. In these examples, Nebuchadnezzar II's conquest of Jerusalem and the kingdom of Judah as well as the deportation of some of the population to Babylon – including the king and the court – are the central topics. The Babylonian Exile ended in 539 BCE, when the Persian king Cyrus II (559–530 BCE) conquered the city and allowed individual groups of people to return home. The destruction of Judah's statehood and the resulting exile was a watershed event in Jewish history and is commemorated

Fig. 54: The European perception of Babylon: "Das babylonische Weib" (The Babylonian Whore) by Albrecht Dürer (1471–1528).

Fig. 55: The inside of this Islamic magic bowl from Iraq is engraved with magic formulas to protect against animal bites and stings, as well as a dragon, a snake, and a scorpion. This bronze bowl dates to the 13th century CE (I.1992.7).

in numerous biblical passages.[26] The Babylonian Exile found its way into popular culture by way of the song "Rivers of Babylon", originally written and recorded by the Jamaican reggae band The Melodians, and later covered by Boney M.

In the New Testament, Babylon appears mainly in the book of Revelation. Here the city is probably a cipher for Rome and the Roman Empire. Babylon is described as "the great" and as the "mother of whores and of earth's abominations" (Revelation 17:5). While the "whore of Babylon" was obviously not a reference to the ancient city, this passage in particular has often served as a model for the depiction of Babylon. The myth of Babylon as a morally depraved city

lives on to this day, for example in the popular TV series *Babylon Berlin*.

Early Islamic scholars were particularly interested in Babylon and painted a more positive picture of the city than the Judeo-Christian tradition. They had a special interest in pre-Islamic history, and travellers visited the ruins over and over again (see p. 40). In the Qur'an itself, Babylon is mentioned only once: Sura 2:102 tells of the angels Harut and Marut trying to instruct the people of Babylon in witchcraft, pointing out the dangers of magical knowledge. According to tradition, God also sent the two angels to earth to resist human temptation. However, they fell for a beautiful woman and then murdered the witness to their misstep. As punishment, these "fallen" angels were held captive and tortured in a well in Babylon. This is the origin of another mythical line of interpretation, according to which Babylon is the city of "witchcraft and wine" (Fig. 55).

In contrast to the accounts transmitted by the monotheistic religions, the works of classical antiquity excessively exalted Babylon (see pp. 38–39). Thus two of the seven wonders of the world were originally located in Babylon: the Hanging Gardens of Semiramis and the city walls of Babylon. These texts also exaggerated the size of the city and its buildings. Thus this strand of tradition also failed to paint a realistic picture of the ancient city, but it did shape the concept of Babylon as shrouded in legend.

THE RECEPTION OF THE ISHTAR GATE – FROM MODERN ART TO SNACK BAR

The colourfully glazed large-scale architectural monuments of Babylon – the Ishtar Gate, the Processional Way, and the Throne Room Façade – have experienced the kind of broad public reception enjoyed by few other ancient Near Eastern artefacts. The wide variety of reproductions of both the entire gate and individual elements of its glazed brick decoration are hard to keep track of and can be found in very different contexts. The spectrum ranges from embroidery patterns and advertisements for snack bars to the interior design of a subway station, from films and comics to modern art.

While Babylon and the stories and protagonists handed down in the Bible have been frequent motifs in European art since the Middle Ages, depictions of the Ishtar Gate can be traced exclusively to the visualisation of the

Fig. 56: The Lion of Babylon, by Walter Andrae, 1899 (VAK 8).

German excavation's findings and the reconstructions in Berlin and Babylon. About a year after the excavation began, the *Deutsche Orient-Gesellschaft* sent reprints of the pictorial reconstruction of the Lion of Babylon to its members (Fig. 56). Together with the other glazed brick façades, these seem to have met with great interest. For example, Friedrich Sarre (1865–1945), the first director of the Berlin *Museum für Islamische Kunst* (Museum of Islamic Art), had a frieze of six Babylonian lions made of glass tiles installed when he built his villa in Babelsberg, Potsdam in 1906 (Fig. 57). Another replica, made in 1913, can be found in the Klosterstraße subway station (in Berlin Mitte), where the walls are decorated with glazed tiles in the style of the Throne Room Façade (Fig. 58). These two imitations of Babylonian glazed brick decoration are thus significantly older than the reconstruction in the Pergamon Museum!

After the museum opened in 1930, visitors could buy postcards and a brochure there, but only in black and white. In 1966, the GDR introduced a series of stamps depicting the bull and the dragon on the Ishtar Gate as well as the lion on the Processional Way and the Throne Room Façade (Fig. 59). Deutsche Post took up the same motif in 2013, with stamps depicting a section of the Ishtar Gate in the Pergamon Museum.

These Babylonian large-scale architectural monuments have also found their way into popular culture and have been depicted in comics, action films, and video games, among other places. The Ishtar Gate, for example, can be seen in Marvel's latest superhero film *Eternals*. Numerous, mostly Arabic shops, restaurants, and snack bars around the world also make use

Fig. 57: The lion frieze at Villa Sarre in Babelsberg, Potsdam, built in 1906.

of the Ishtar Gate, the lions, or the rosette motifs (Figs. 61 and 63).

In addition to official depictions, for example on banknotes and paintings featuring Saddam Hussein, the Ishtar Gate was and still is very present in Iraq today. Even at Baghdad International Airport, travellers are greeted by a replica of the Ishtar Gate (Fig. 62). The motifs can be found as graffiti on the streets of Baghdad, in amusement park designs, in church decorations, or as posters in private living rooms. Furthermore, various Iraqi embassies – such as those in Amman, Manama, and Beijing – are designed in the style of the Ishtar Gate.

In recent years, various contemporary artists have grappled with the Ishtar Gate, and their work has reflected on it in different ways. The American sculptor and painter Robert Reynolds created two works after his visit to the Pergamon Museum in 2006, in which he transferred the Ishtar Gate and the Throne Room Façade to different media: *"Ishtar Chariot of Nebuchad-*

Fig. 58: The 1913 replica of the Throne Room Façade in the Klosterstraße subway station (Berlin Mitte).

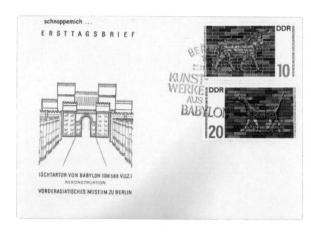

Fig. 59: Mail from the Pergamon Museum: First Day Cover of an edition of collector's stamps, 1966.

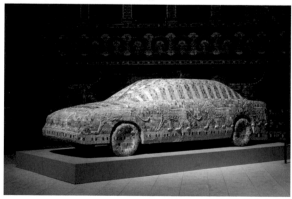

Fig. 60: Robert Reynolds's *"Ishtar Chariot of Nebuchadnezzar II"* in the Pergamon Museum (2006).

Fig. 61: Window display at a men's outfitter in Damascus (2003).

Fig. 62: The Meeting Point at Baghdad International Airport (2018).

Fig. 63: Babylon Restaurant in Bielefeld (2019).

Fig. 64: The art book *The God Marduk*, by Hanna Malallah (2008)

nezzar II" is a car decorated with the motifs of the Throne Room Façade (Fig. 60), while *"The Dragon of Marduk"* is a three-dimensional steel and ceramic transposition of the snake-dragon from the Ishtar Gate. Both works directly relate to the reconstructions and feature the characteristic seams between the bricks.

The cover of an art book by the Iraqi painter Hanna Malallah also depicts the snake-dragon. In her 2008 work entitled *The God Marduk*, the artist addressed the fragility and destruction of Iraq's cultural heritage (Fig. 64). The American artist Michael Rakowitz, who comes from a Jewish-Iraqi family, also explores this theme. His work focuses on the looting of the Iraq Museum in 2003 and the ongoing destruction of cultural heritage in Iraq. In his best-known work, "The invisible enemy should not exist" (2007 to the present), the title of which calls up the ancient name of the Processional Way, he reconstructs ancient Near Eastern artworks out of everyday objects, such as Middle Eastern packaging and Arabic newspapers. In 2010, under the title "May the arrogant not prevail", he reconstructed the Ishtar Gate out of packaging material. "May the arrogant not prevail" is another translation of the name of the processional street, *Ay-ibūr-shāpû*.

---

25 The abbreviation Tanakh is derived from the initial letters of the three main components of the Hebrew Bible: Torah (law), Nevi'im (prophets), and Ketuvim (writings).

26 The most important passages on Babylon in the Hebrew Bible/Old Testament are 2 Kings 24:20–25:21; Jeremiah 52:1–23; Ezra 1:1–6; and 2 Chronicles 36:11–21. For a concise summary of Babylon in the biblical tradition, see Seymour 2016: 35–51; see also the contributions by Herrmann and Kratz in Marzahn and Schauerte 2008.

APPENDIX

DEFINITIONS OF KEY TERMS

The key terms and persons listed below appear several times in the main text. While the textboxes above explain some of these terms and figures in detail, certain key terms are briefly expounded here to promote better understanding.

Adad was the Babylonian weather god responsible for rain, storms, and thunderstorms. In areas dependent upon rain-fed agriculture, he ensured the harvest, but he also endangered it with storms, floods, and droughts. People in the ancient Near East also worshipped other weather gods in addition to Adad. Apart from a bolt of lightning, which Adad was often depicted holding in his hand, he was also represented by the lion-dragon, and in Babylonia particularly by the bull.
For the *akītu* festival, see the textbox on pp. 30–31.

Akkadian is a Semitic language related to Hebrew and Arabic. Of this group of languages, it is the oldest one attested in writing. Akkadian is a modern collective term that includes Babylonian and Assyrian, in addition to other dialects. We have written evidence of Akkadian from the middle of the 3rd millennium BCE until the 1st century CE. The extent and diversity of its textual tradition make Akkadian the most important representative of ancient Near Eastern languages.

Assyria refers to the territory of the Assyrian Empire (see the entry below); the name originates with the capital city, Ashur. In a narrower sense, it refers to the core Assyrian area between the cities of Ashur, Nineveh (present-day Mosul), and Arbail (present-day Erbil) in northern Iraq. In a broader sense, Assyria is used to refer to the whole of northern Mesopotamia (what is today northern Iraq and eastern Syria) or as a designation for the Assyrian Empire. After the fall of the empire, Assyria lived on as a regional and provincial designation in the Persian, Hellenistic, and Roman periods.

The **Assyrian Empire** was a kingdom in what is now northern Iraq. It is named after its capital city, Ashur, (today Qal'at Sherqat). The city was inhabited from the middle of the 3rd millennium BCE at the latest. At the beginning of the 2nd millennium BCE, the city-state had an extensive trade network, which also included settlements in Anatolia (the Old Assyrian period). Over the following centuries, the city was temporarily part of the Mittani kingdom. In the 14th century BCE, the Assyrians regained their independence and established a territorial state in northern Mesopotamia (the Middle Assyrian kingdom, in what is today northern Iraq and Syria). From the 9th century BCE, Assyria rose to become a great power (the Neo-Assyrian Empire). In the 8th and 7th centuries BCE, the Assyrian kings ruled all of the Near East, including Babylonia and even Egypt. At the end of the 7th century, the huge empire collapsed in the course of just a few years, and Babylonia became the dominant power in Mesopotamia.

Babylonia is used today as both a geographical and a political designation. Named after its former capital city, Babylon, southern Mesopotamia – what is today southern Iraq – is referred to as Babylonia. The Babylonians themselves called the area *māt akkadî* ("the land of Akkad"). People in Hellenistic and Roman times used the term Babylonia, taken from ancient Greek, for different areas of present-day (southern) Iraq, and the name has been handed down ever since. In addition, Babylonia often stands for the Babylonian Empire (see the entry below).

The term **Babylonian Empire** basically refers to the territorial dominion originating from the city of Babylon. Over the course of its eventful history, various dynasties ruled over the city (see pp. 8–11). Babylonian Empire usually refers to one of the two periods of prosperity when the city enjoyed supra-regional importance. This refers either to the Old Babylonian kingdom (ca. 1800–1595 BCE) under the First Babylonian Dynasty (see the entry on Hammurabi) or the Neo-Babylonian Empire (626–539 BCE) under Nabopolassar and his successors (see the text box on Nebuchadnezzar II, pp. 14–15).

Clay tablets were the most common medium for writing in cuneiform (see the entry below). Scribes formed tablets from moist clay and wrote on them with a stylus. They made these clay tablets in very different sizes and shapes (rectangular, square, round, and oval), depending on the time period and the content. In addition to clay, scribes in the ancient Near East used other materials such as stone, metal, or wax for writing.

Cuneiform is a script named after the characteristic shape of its signs, which scribes pressed into moist clay with a stylus. This writing system originated in southern Mesopotamia in the late 4th millennium BCE. The people who invented this script probably spoke Sumerian (see the entry below). Scribes later used cuneiform to write other languages in Mesopotamia and neighbouring areas. Until the middle of the 1st millennium BCE, cuneiform was the predominant writing system in the region. Subsequently the alphabetic scripts (Phoenician/Punic, Aramaic, Hebrew, and Greek), which were easier to learn, increasingly prevailed.

The **Deutsche Orient-Gesellschaft** (German Oriental Society or DOG) is a scholarly association founded in 1898 for the study of Near Eastern cultures and the acquisition of objects for the Berlin museums. The association still exists today and continues to promote research into and propagation of ancient Near Eastern cultures.

Division of finds/Partage refers to an arrangement in which the finds from an excavation are divided between the country of origin and the foreign excavators. Such divisions of finds were common practice in the 19th and early 20th centuries and were regulated by the antiquities laws of the respective countries. In individual cases, the countries of provenance divided up the finds afterwards – for example, to create incentives for excavators to participate in emergency excavations to investigate endangered ruins. From today's perspective, the divisions of finds that took place in asymmetrical or quasi-colonial contexts is viewed through a critical lens, as the countries of origin often lacked sovereignty over their own cultural heritage.

Hammurabi (which means "the father's brother/paternal uncle is a healer") reigned as king in Babylon from about 1792 to 1750 BCE. He was the fifth ruler of Babylon's First Dynasty, succeeding his father Sin-muballit to the throne. Under Hammurabi, Babylon developed from a local power into the foremost kingdom of Mesopotamia, and the maximum extent of its territory stretched from the Persian Gulf in the south to eastern Syria in the north and the Zagros Mountains in the east. His ideas about law and royal rule have been handed down in the famous Code of Hammurabi, which is now housed in the Louvre (Fig. 2).

For **Ishtar**, see the textbox on p. 27.

Marduk was the city god of Babylon. He became increasingly important as Babylon developed from a city-state into a great kingdom. Over the course of the 2nd millennium BCE, he became Babylon's supreme deity, and people throughout Mesopotamia worshipped him. At that time, people usually referred to him simply as *Bēl* (Akkadian for "lord"), a term which underlines his supreme position. According to the Babylonian worldview, Marduk's shrine *Esangil* ("house whose head is high") in Babylon was the centre of the cosmos. Marduk was associated with the spade and the snake-dragon *Mušhuššu* (see the entry below).

Mesopotamia, which comes from the ancient Greek word meaning "land between the rivers", is an ancient name for the area around the Tigris and Euphrates rivers. The region is bordered by the Zagros and Tarus mountains, the Persian Gulf, and the Syrian desert. Mesopotamia corresponds to the present-day territories of Iraq and parts of Iran, Turkey, Syria, and Kuwait.

Mušhuššu was an ancient Near Eastern hybrid creature. The Sumerian name *Mušhuššu* means "fearsome or furious snake". The dragon-like creature had a snake's head, the forelegs of a lion, the hind legs of a bird of prey, and a scorpion's stinging tail. From the 3rd millennium BCE, *Mušhuššu* represented various Mesopotamian deities. Beginning in Hammurabi's time, the creature came to represent the Babylonian state god Marduk.

The **Near East** refers to the south-western part of the continent of Asia. Other terms used for the region are Eastern Mediterranean and Middle East. The terms Near East and Eastern Mediterranean also include Egypt and Cyprus, to some extent. All three terms refer to the region in terms of its relationship to Europe, which is why scholars now often use the more neutral terms West Asia and Southwest Asia in academic publications. For clarity and east of understanding, we have retained the established term Near East in this volume.

For **Nebuchadnezzar II,** see the textbox on pp. 14–15.

For the **New Year festival,** see the textbox on pp. 30–31.

The **Orient** (from the Latin *sol oriens*, meaning "rising sun") was originally one of the four regions of the Roman world. Today the term usually refers to the Arab–Islamic influenced area of the Near East. In his seminal work on Orientalism, Edward Said (1978) argued that "Orient" and "Occident" are Eurocentric concepts that express the West's sense of superiority over the "Orient". We therefore generally avoid using the term

Orient in this volume and only use it with reference to this stereotypical Western image of the "Orient". For a more differentiated presentation of the term Orient(alism), see al-Otaibi 2006, with further references.

Sumerian was a language native to southern Mesopotamia and is not related to any language known to us today. It is one of the so-called dead languages and has been handed down in the form of cuneiform texts that most likely date to the end of the 4th millennium BCE (proto-cuneiform), but at the latest from 2,700 until the end of the 1st millennium BCE. Sumerian disappeared as a spoken language sometime around the transition from the 3rd to the 2nd millennium BCE. Subsequently people only used it as a written language in the literary and cultic spheres.

The **Vorderasiatische Abteilung** (Department of the Ancient Near East, known since 1948 as the *Vorderasiatisches Museum* or Museum of the Ancient Near East) of the Royal Museums in Berlin (from 1918/19 the *Staatliche Museen* or National Museums of Berlin) was founded in 1899. Prior to this, the collection of ancient Near Eastern objects had been scattered across other departments among the Royal Museums. After the Near Eastern antiquities were initially displayed in various buildings on Museum Island, the *Vorderasiatische Abteilung* was given its own permanent exhibition in the Pergamon Museum beginning in 1930.

BIBLIOGRAPHY (FURTHER READING LISTED BY CHAPTER)

The City of Babylon

Beaulieu, Paul-Alain (2018). *A History of Babylon, 2200 BC–AD 75*. Hoboken, NJ: John Wiley & Sons Ltd (Blackwell history of the ancient world).

Cancik-Kirschbaum, Eva, Margarete van Ess, and Joachim Marzahn (eds.) (2011). *Babylon: Wissenskultur in Orient und Okzident. Babylon*. Berlin: De Gruyter.

Dalley, Stephanie (2021). *The City of Babylon: A History, c. 2000 BC – AD 116*. Cambridge: Cambridge University Press.

Finkel, Irving L. and Michael Seymour (eds.) (2009). *Babylon: Myth and Reality*. London: British Museum Press.

George, A. R. (1992). *Babylonian Topographical Texts*. Leuven: Peeters.

Marzahn, Joachim and Günther Schauerte (eds.) (2008). *Babylon. Wahrheit*. Munich: Hirmer.

Pedersén, Olof (2021). *Babylon. The Great City*. Münster: Zaphon.

Radner, Karen (2020). *A Short History of Babylon*. London: Bloomsbury Academic.

The Ishtar Gate, the Processional Way, and the Throne Room Façade

Amrhein, Anastasia, Clare Fitzgerald, and Elizabeth Knott (eds.) (2020). *A Wonder to Behold: Craftsmanship and the Creation of Babylon's Ishtar Gate*. Princeton: Princeton University Press.

Koldewey, Robert (1918). *Das Ischtar-Tor in Babylon*. Leipzig: Hinrichs (Wissenschaftliche Veröffentlichung der Deutschen Orient-Gesellschaft 32).

Koldewey, Robert (1931). *Die Königsburgen von Babylon 1. Die Südburg*. Leipzig: Hinrichs (Wissenschaftliche Veröffentlichung der Deutschen Orient-Gesellschaft 54).

Marzahn, Joachim (1995). *The Ishtar Gate. The Processional Way. The New Year Festival of Babylon*. Mainz: Philipp v. Zabern.

Pedersén, Olof (2018). "The Ishtar Gate Area in Babylon. From Old Documents to New Interpretations in a Digital Model." *Zeitschrift für Orient-Archäologie* 11, pp. 160–178.

Pedersén, Olof (2020). "The Glazed Bricks that Ornamented Babylon – A Short Overview." In: *Glazed Brick Decoration in the Ancient Near East: Proceedings of a Workshop at the 11th International Congress of the Archaeology of the Ancient Near East (Munich) in April 2018*. Edited by Anja Fügert and Helen Gries. Oxford: Archaeopress, pp. 96–122.

Thavapalan, Shiyanthi (2020). *The Meaning of Color in Ancient Mesopotamia*. Leiden/Boston: Brill.

Watanabw, Chikako E. (2015). "The Symbolic Role of Animals in Babylon. A Contextual Approach to the Lion, the Bull and the Mušḫuššu." *Iraq* 77, pp. 215–224.

Exploring Babylon

Andrae, Walter (1952). *Babylon: Die versunkene Weltstadt und ihr Ausgräber Robert Koldewey*. Berlin: De Gruyter.

Beigel, Thorsten, and Sabine Mangold (eds.) (2017). *Wilhelm II: Archäologie und Politik um 1900*. Stuttgart: Franz Steiner Verlag.

Finkel, Irving L. (ed.) (2013). *The Cyrus Cylinder: The King*

of Persia's Proclamation from Ancient Babylon. London/New York: I.B. Tauris.

Henkelman, Wouter, Amélie Kuhrt, Robert Rollinger, and Josef Wiesehöfer (2011). "Herodotus and Babylon Reconsidered." In: *Herodot und das Persische Weltreich. Herodotus and the Persian Empire.* Edited by Robert Rollinger, Brigitte Truschnegg, and Reinhold Bichler. Wiesbaden: Harrassowitz (Classica et Orientalia 3), pp. 449–470.

Jacobs, Bruno (2011). "Ktesias und die Architektur Babylons." In: *Die Welt des Ktesias/Ctesias' World.* Edited by Josef Wiesehöfer, Robert Rollinger, and Giovanni B. Lanfranchi. Wiesbaden: Harrassowitz (Classica et Orientalia 1), pp. 141–157.

Kohlmeyer, Kay, Eva Strommenger, and Hansjörg Schmid (1991). *Wiedererstehendes Babylon: eine antike Weltstadt im Blick der Forschung.* Berlin: Museum für Vor- und Frühgeschichte der Staatlichen Museen Preußischer Kulturbesitz.

Koldewey, Robert (1914). *The Excavations at Babylon.* London: Macimillian and Co.

Kuyt, Annelies (2003). "Die Welt aus sefardischer und ashkenazischer Sicht: Die mittelalterlichen hebräischen Reiseberichte des Benjamin von Tudela und des Petachja von Regensburg." In: *Zur Poetik der Reise- und Länderberichte. Vorträge eines interdisziplinären Symposiums vom 19. bis 24. Juni 2000 an der Justus-Liebig-Universität Gießen.* Edited by Xenja von Ertzdorff and Gerhard Giesemann. Amsterdam: Rodopi, pp. 211–231.

Matthes, Olaf (2000). *James Simon. Mäzen im Wilhelminischen Zeitalter.* Edited by Thomas Gaehtgens, Jürgen Kocka, and Reinhard Rürup. Berlin: B & S Siebenhaar Verlag.

Matthes, Olaf (2000). „Zur Vorgeschichte der deutschen Ausgrabungen in Babylon." In: *Babylon: Focus mesopotamischer Geschichte, Wiege früher Gelehrsamkeit, Mythos in der Moderne.* Edited by Johannes Renger. Saarbrücken: SDV (Internationales Colloquium der Deutschen Orient-Gesellschaft 2), pp. 33–45.

al-Otaibi, Fahad M. (2006). "Towards a Contrapuntal Reading of History: Orientalism and the Ancient Near East." *Journal of King Saud University – Arts* 19, pp. 55–66.

Quatember, Ursula, and Hansgeorg Bankel (eds.) (2018). *Post aus Babylon: Robert Koldewey, Bauforscher und Ausgräber. Briefe aus Kleinasien, Italien, Deutschland und dem Vorderen Orient von 1882 bis 1922.* Vienna: Phoibos Verlag.

Rollinger, Robert (2013). "Berossos and the Monuments: City Walls, Sanctuaries, Palaces and the Hanging Garden." In: *The World of Berossos: Proceedings of the 4th International Colloquium on "The Ancient Near East between Classical and Ancient Oriental Traditions", Hatfield College, Durham 7th –9th July 2010.* Edited by Johannes Haubold, Giovanni B. Lanfranchi, Robert Rollinger, and John Steele. Wiesbaden: Harrassowitz (Classica et orientalia 5), pp. 137–162.

Said, Edward W. (1979). *Orientalism.* New York: Vintage.

Thelle, Rannfrid I. (2020). *Discovering Babylon.* London: Routledge.

Trümpler, Charlotte (ed.) (2008). *Das grosse Spiel: Archäologie und Politik zur Zeit des Kolonialismus (1860–1940).* Cologne: DuMont.

Vorderasiatisches Museum (ed.) (2000). *Vorderasiatisches Museum Berlin: Geschichte und Geschichten zum hundertjährigen Bestehen.* Berlin: Staatl. Museen zu Berlin, Preußischer Kulturbesitz.

Wartke, Ralf-Bernhard (ed.) (2008). *Auf dem Weg nach Babylon: Robert Koldewey, ein Archäologenleben.* Mainz: Philipp von Zabern.

From Babylon to Berlin

Andrae, Walter (1961). *Lebenserinnerungen eines Ausgräbers.* Edited by Kurt Bittel and Ernst Heinrich. Berlin: De Gruyter.

Andrae, Walter, and Rainer Michael Boehmer (1989). *Sketches by an Excavator.* Berlin: Mann.

Collins, Paul, and Charles Tripp (eds.) (2017). *Gertrude Bell and Iraq: A Life and Legacy.* Oxford/New York: Published for the British Academy by Oxford University Press (Proceedings of the British Academy).

Crüsemann, Nicola (2001). *Vom Zweistromland zum Kupfergraben: Vorgeschichte und Entstehungsjahre (1899–1918) der Vorderasiatischen Abteilung der Berliner Museen vor fach- und kulturpolitischen Hintergründen.* Berlin: Gebr. Mann Verlag (Jahrbuch der Berliner Museen, supplement 42).

Eldem, Edhem (2010a). "An Ottoman Archaeologist Caught between Two Worlds: Osman Hamdi Bey (1842–1910)." In: *Archaeology, Anthropology and Heritage in the Balkans and Anatolia: The Life and Times of F. W. Hasluck, 1878–1920.* Edited by David Shankland. Piscataway, NY: Gorgias Press, pp. 121–149.

Eldem, Edhem (2010c). *Un Ottoman en Orient. Osman Hamdi Bey en Irak, 1869–1871.* Arles: Actes Sud.

Eldem, Edhem (2011). "From Blissful Indifference to Anguished Concern: Ottoman Perceptions of Antiquities, 1799–1869." In: *Scramble for the Past: A Story of Archaeology in the Ottoman Empire, 1753–1914*. Edited by Zainab Bahrani, Zeynep Çelik, and Edhem Eldem. Istanbul: SALT, pp. 281–329.

Seydewitz, Nicole (ed.) (2013). *KunstKeramik der Moderne: zum 150. Geburtstag des Veltener Ofen- und Keramikunternehmers Richard Blumenfeld*. Velten: Veltener Verlagsgesellschaft (Baustein: Schriftenreihe des Ofen- und Keramikmuseums Velten).

Winnicke, Winfried (1992). "Märkische Ton-Kunst. Die Oranienburger Werkstätten." In: *Berlin und Brandenburg: Keramik der 20er und 30er Jahre*. Edited by Heinz-Joachim Theis. Stuttgart: Edition Cantz, pp. 43–45.

Tripp, Charles (2007). *A History of Iraq*. 3rd ed. Cambridge: Cambridge University Press.

The Significance and Preservation of a Piece of World Cultural Heritage

Bahrani, Zainab (1998). "Conjuring Mesopotamia: Imaginative Geography and a World Past." In: *Archaeology Under Fire: Nationalism, Politics and Heritage in the Eastern Mediterranean and Middle East*. Edited by Lynn Meskell. London/New York: Routledge, pp. 159–174.

Bahrani, Zainab (2008). "The Battle for Babylon." In: *The Destruction of Cultural Heritage in Iraq*. Edited by Peter G. Stone, Joanne Farchakh Bajjaly, and Robert Fisk. Woodbridge, Suffolk: Boydell Press (The Heritage Matters Series), pp. 165–171.

Baram, Amatzia (1991). *Culture, History, and Ideology in the Formation of Ba'thist Iraq, 1968–89*. New York: St. Martin's Press.

Bernhardsson, Magnus Thorkell (2005). *Reclaiming a Plundered Past: Archaeology and Nation Building in Modern Iraq*. Austin: University of Texas Press.

Kathem, Mehiyar, and Dhiaa Kareem Ali (2020). "Decolonising Babylon." *International Journal of Heritage Studies* 26, pp. 1–15.

Musa, Maryam U. (2011). "The Situation of the Babylon Archaeological Site until 2006." In: *Babylon: Wissenskultur in Orient und Okzident*. Edited by Eva Cancik-Kirschbaum, Margarete van Ess, and Joachim Marzahn. Berlin: De Gruyter, pp. 19–46.

Radujkovic, Sonja (2017). "Von Wasserbädern und Überzügen – aus der Konservierungsgeschichte des Ischtar-Tores im Vorderasiatischen Museum." *Berliner Beiträge zur Archäometrie, Kunsttechnologie und Konservierungswissenschaft* 25, pp. 103–117.

Impact and Reception

Haffner, Dorothee (2019). "Babylonische Löwen: Rezeption und Wanderungen." In: *Von analogen und digitalen Zugängen zur Kunst: Festschrift für Hubertus Kohle zum 60. Geburtstag*. Edited by Maria Effinger et al. Heidelberg: arthistoricum.net, pp. 203–214.

Janssen, Caroline (1995). *Bābil, the City of Witchcraft and Wine: the Name and Fame of Babylon in Medieval Arabic Geographical Texts*. Ghent: University of Ghent (Mesopotamian History and Environment Series 2).

Müller, Hannelore, and Walter Sommerfeld (2010). "Von der Welthauptstadt zum Weltkulturerbe – Eine Nachlese zur Stadtgeschichte von Babylon." In: *Zwischen Orient und Okzident: Studien zu Mobilität von Wissen, Konzepten und Praktiken*. Edited by Anke Bentzin, Henner Fürtig, Thomas Krüppner, and Riem Spielhaus. Freiburg: Herder, pp. 268–288.

Polaschegg, Andrea, and Michael Weichenhan (eds.) (2017). *Berlin–Babylon: Eine deutsche Faszination 1890–1930*. Berlin: Verlag Klaus Wagenbach.

Seymour, Michael (2016). *Babylon. Legend, History and the Ancient City*. London/New York: I.B. Tauris.

Verderame, L., and Agnès Garcia-Ventura (eds.) (2020). *Receptions of the Ancient Near East in Popular Culture and Beyond*. Atlanta, GA: Lockwood Press.

Wullen, Moritz (ed.) (2008). *Mythos*. Munich: Hirmer.

COPYRIGHTS

dation, Foto: Latif al Ani • Figs. 34, 35, 36 © Staatliche Museen zu Berlin, Vorderasiatisches Museum / Deutsche Orient-Gesellschaft, Foto: Walter Andrae • Fig. 37 Historic Collection/ Alamy Stock Foto, Bild-ID: KJY7X4 • Fig. 39 bpk / Nationalgalerie, SMB / Bernd Kuhnert • Fig. 38 © Gertrude Bell Archive, Newcastle University • Figs. 27, 40, 41, 42, 43, 44, 46, 47 © Staatliche Museen zu Berlin, Vorderasiatisches Museum, Fotograf unbekannt • Fig. 43 © Saatsbibliothek zu Berlin – Preußischer Kulturbesitz, Nachl. Walter Andrae 238, Nr. 1, Foto: Ruth Schacht • Fig. 48 © Staatliche Museen zu Berlin, Vorderasiatisches Museum, Foto: Willy Römer • Fig. 50 *Iraq State Board for Antiquities and Heritage* • Figg. 51, 62 Foto: Karen Radner • Fig. 54, bpk / Kupferstichkabinett, SMB / Dietmar Katz • Fig. 55 © Staatliche Museen zu Berlin, Museum für Islamische Kunst, Foto: Christian Krug • Fig. 57 Foto: Ralf-B. Wartke • Figs. 61, 63 Foto: Nadja Cholidis.

ACKNOWLEDGEMENTS

My special thanks go to Nadja Cholidis, Barbara Helwing, and Daniel López-Kuczmik, who supported this creation in many ways and shared their knowledge with me. I am grateful to Pınar Durgun, Christopher Hölzel, Elisabeth Katzy, Joachim Marzahn, Lutz Martin, Olof Pedersén, Sonja Radujkovic, Julia Rummel, Giulia Russo, Nicole Seydewitz and Thomas Tunsch for hints, suggestions, and corrections. Ilsemarie Shawa kindly took on the proofreading. Olaf M. Teßmer and Alrun Gutow assisted me with photo research and image data management. I extend my gratitude to Virginie Fabre, Hanna Malallah, Martina Müller-Wiener, Karen Radner, Daniel Schwemer, Ariane Thomas, and Ralf-B. Wartke for their kind permission to reprint certain images. Finally, my thanks go to Marika Mäder, Sigrid Wollmeiner, and Isabell Schlott for their professional and committed supervision of the publication.

Bibliographic information published by the Deutsche Nationalbibliothek:
The Deutsche Nationalbibliothek lists this publication in the Deutsche Nationalbibliografie; detailed bibliographic data are available on the Internet at: http://dnb.dnb.de.

First edition 2022
© 2022 Staatliche Museen zu Berlin – Preußischer Kulturbesitz / Verlag Schnell & Steiner GmbH, Leibnizstraße 13, 93055 Regensburg
Publication management for the museums: Marika Mäder, Sigrid Wollmeiner
Translator: Alissa Jones Nelson
Cover Design: Anna Braungart, Tübingen
Cover: © Staatliche Museen zu Berlin – Vorderasiatisches Museum, Photo: Olaf M. Teßmer
Layout: typegerecht berlin
Print: Gutenberg Beuys Feindruckerei GmbH, Langenhagen
ISBN 978-3-7954-3726-8

Further information about our publications can be found under: www.schnell-und-steiner.de
www.smb.museum